Writer/Designer

A Guide to Making Multimodal Projects

Writer/Designer

A Guide to Making Multimodal Projects

Kristin L. Arola
Washington State University

Jennifer Sheppard
New Mexico State University

Cheryl E. Ball
West Virginia University

Bedford/St. Martin's
Boston | New York

For Bedford/St. Martin's

Publisher for Composition: Leasa Burton
Developmental Editor: Sophia Snyder
Assistant Production Editor: Laura Clark
Assistant Production Manager: Joe Ford
Executive Marketing Manager: Molly Parke
Editorial Assistant: Rachel Childs
Copy Editor: Arthur Johnson
Indexer: Jake Kawatski
Photo Researcher: Rona Tuccillo
Text Design: Books By Design, Inc.
Cover Design: Marine Miller
Composition: Books By Design, Inc.
Printing and Binding: RR Donnelley and Sons

President, Bedford/St. Martin's: Denise B. Wydra
Editorial Director for English and Music: Karen S. Henry
Director of Marketing: Karen R. Soeltz
Production Director: Susan W. Brown
Director of Rights and Permissions: Hilary Newman

Manufactured in China

8   7   6
f   e

For information, write: Bedford/St. Martin's, 75 Arlington Street, Boston, MA 02116   (617-399-4000)

ISBN 978-1-4576-0045-6 (Student Edition)
ISBN 978-1-4576-6409-0 (Instructor's Edition)

Preface for Instructors

Working with multimodal texts can bring up lots of questions for both students and instructors. What's the best way to get students started with a multimodal project? Is it necessary to learn a lot of new technologies? How do you assess multimodal work, anyway? In *Writer/Designer*, we aim to help you answer these questions, making multimodal composing strategies and projects accessible to you and your students. We know how to help you through it because we've been there—throughout the book, you'll be learning from the successes, mistakes, and experiences we've had teaching, supervising, and creating multimodal work.

The title of this book, *Writer/Designer: A Guide to Making Multimodal Projects*, reflects our belief that writing and designing always work together. Whether authors are working with words, images, sound, or movement, decisions about what content says and how it looks and functions are necessarily entwined, even when we don't pay conscious attention to their relationship. We want our students to always be aware of how writing and designing work together, to think of themselves as equal parts writers and designers. Both design and content influence how audiences respond to a text's message, so developing familiarity with design practices as well as textual composition is critical for successful communication. This book helps students to develop these skills together, providing them with a rhetorical toolkit for making purposeful, relevant choices in their writing and designing.

We know from our own professional experiences and those of colleagues who share our pedagogical interests that integrating multimodal projects into our teaching can often lead to feeling like we are "ambassadors of multimodality" for our students, programs, and departments. Each of us has experienced the need to justify the significance of our multimodal pedagogies and what they offer to students' preparation for academic and professional life. Although the focus of *Writer/Designer* is on helping students develop compositional and rhetorical strategies, we also provide explanations of multimodality's value that will be of use to instructors who need to make the case that facility with diverse literacies and modalities will strengthen students' rhetorical and communicative skills. The book's clear, accessible guidance for teaching multimodal composition may help ambassadors discuss multimodal pedagogy with writing program administrators, department heads, colleagues, and teaching assistants. Further rationales on the value and significance of multimodality can be found in the Instructor's Manual's annotated bibliography.

Multimodality and Genres and Life

Whether at school, on the job, or just in everyday life, multimodal texts have become an essential part of communication in nearly every arena of contemporary culture. The widespread use of design and media software, Web 2.0 technologies, and other digital media has increased opportunities to convey information and has also changed the expectations of readers. We wrote this book specifically to help authors learn how to make conscious multimodal choices in the texts they create, no matter what mode, medium, or rhetorical situation they are working in. With the guidance and activities we've provided in *Writer/ Designer*, authors—your students—will be more prepared for the complex rhetorical challenges they face as students and future professionals.

We designed this book to support the integration of multimodal projects into classrooms through both short-term and semester-long projects. The book offers accessible strategies for composing with multiple modes of communication, including detailed examples and explanations of what multimodality means, rationales for why multimodality matters, and in-depth support for how to compose multimodal projects within a variety of contexts. The chapters use a mix of student-produced and real-world projects to illustrate the rhetorical choices and strategies discussed.

Grounded in Theory, Supported in Practice

While we organized this book to lead authors through a chronological process in analyzing, planning, and designing multimodal texts, we also kept it brief and flexible enough to meet any instructor's individual needs and personal expertise. In addition, the assignments we've included can support authors in creating their own projects in any genre or situation. *Writer/Designer* is meant to be easy to use in any number of courses across disciplines, either on its own or bundled with your favorite textbook or handbook.

This book is grounded in our own praxes, pedagogies, and theoretical leanings. We are particularly influenced by the New London Group (NLG)—a group of literacy scholars who make the deceptively simple argument that "literacy pedagogy must now account for the burgeoning variety of text forms associated with information and multimedia technologies." Their work makes the case that such pedagogies more richly prepare students for the diverse rhetorical and communicative practices they need to succeed as students, as professionals, and as citizens in the twenty-first century.

As friends in graduate school in the early 2000s, we were immersed in the NLG's pedagogy of multiliteracies when it was used by our writing program faculty to reimagine the first-year writing course we all taught. Rather than concentrating exclusively on written text, we were introduced to a model of composition instruction that focused on integrating written, oral, and visual communication. This curriculum helped students learn to craft texts in a variety of modes and genres to best meet their diverse rhetorical needs.

In the years since our first experiences in that multimodal classroom, we've gone on to specialize in different areas of rhetoric and writing studies, but the theory and pedagogy of what we experienced in those early days continue to influence our work today. Kristin leads a program focused on the intersections of digital technology and culture; Jenny runs the Design Center at New Mexico State University, where she supports students' hands-on production of print and digital media for campus and community clients; Cheryl's work as editor of the journal *Kairos* helps our field rethink how scholarship about digital writing can be modeled in digital forms. As we've developed and refined syllabi in a variety of courses, created our own multimodal projects, and mentored authors through their composition processes, we've discovered a series of best practices, backed up by theory, that we want to share with you. This book benefits from our collective experiences and builds from many of the assignments and syllabi we've designed. You can see some of these syllabi and other curricular materials in the Instructor's Manual.

One of the biggest lessons we've learned is the value of learning-by-doing through writing for authentic audiences and purposes (what the New London Group would call "situated practice"). Incorporating multimodal composition projects into the classroom provides valuable avenues for students to explore all available means of persuasion for communicating their ideas in any rhetorical situation. Learning to communicate persuasively in any situation requires sustained opportunities to practice this kind of composition, in addition to an awareness of general rhetorical strategies and the affordances offered by different media and modalities. Providing students with the chance to experiment and reflect on composing in different modalities will help them develop the confidence and competence they need to leverage both old and new technologies and media for successful communication.

Additionally, the examples and processes discussed in this book draw from both classroom and real-world texts to help students see how multimodality works in a variety of contexts and genres. We provide tools for critically analyzing available resources, as well as for understanding how different modes can be brought together in creative and complex ways to convey new meanings across multiple, new situations. Research in rhetorical genre studies suggests that this method of recursive analysis and production, specifically done within genres that are found in everyday life, helps authors learn how to write in multiple situations. The Instructor's Manual offers an annotated bibliography that covers issues of rhetorical genre studies, multiliteracies, multimodal composition, and more.

Features of the Book and How to Use Them

- **A process-focused approach** introduces and illustrates foundational concepts while tying them to the practices students will actually use in creating their projects. Real multimodal texts by students and professionals, included in e-Pages, an online section of every chapter, inspire students and model what's possible.

- **Bedford Integrated Media with e-Pages**, which you and your students can access at **bedfordstmartins.com/writerdesigner**, help us illustrate a wider variety of media and design choices than we can in a printed book. The e-Pages include online material that furthers student learning through interactive texts and additional Process! activities. These examples help students unpack the rhetorical and design decisions that have gone into creating multimodal texts. In addition, the e-Pages for this book include the full version of *ix: visualizing composition*, a digital resource that provides hands-on, interactive tutorials for analyzing and applying 13 rhetorically based design elements.

- **Write/Design** assignments help students dig into chapter concepts and scaffold students' development of larger-scale projects. They ask students to complete process-focused activities such as a rhetorical analysis of several multimodal texts of their choosing, an annotated source list, or a draft of the storyboards/mock-ups they'll use to organize their multimodal projects.

- **Process!** activities pose questions that ask students to practice their skills and reflect on their understanding of the chapter content. These activities appear throughout each chapter and prepare authors to apply concepts from the book to either sample multimedia texts or their own projects. Process! activities teach students about practices such as analyzing modal affordances, conceptualizing project designs, learning about fair use and different kinds of Creative Commons licenses, and brainstorming dos and don'ts lists for successful collaboration.

- **Case Studies** highlight and analyze actual (published or presented) examples of multimodal texts. In case studies, we provide in-depth analyses of an author's composing processes that correspond to the stage of writing/designing outlined in that chapter. Case studies also showcase how the design vocabulary or concepts we present in each chapter are put into practice in the design process. Example texts from case studies include a rhetorical and design analysis of a university Web site, a student's annotated storyboard for a short film, and a designer's revision process for a magazine cover.

- **Sidebars** offer short additional explanations and insights about the material covered in the text. Sidebars elaborate on key concepts (such as "Are

All Texts Multimodal?"), provide more detailed discussion on issues like designing for access, and offer guidance on different aspects of the multimodal composing process (such as strategies for working alone rather than with a team) that may apply only to certain projects.

Whether you are new to teaching multimodal projects or someone who has lots of experience, we designed this book to give your students a strong foundation in the concepts and practices of multimodal composing. You'll also find the additional materials in the Instructor's Manual helpful. In it, we've compiled more assignments, syllabi, and supporting content to provide further ideas on integrating multimodality into your writing classes.

Acknowledgments

This book would never have been possible without the guidance and support of the people we worked with at Bedford/St. Martin's. In particular, we'd like to thank Joan Feinberg, co-president of Macmillan Higher Education; Denise Wydra, president of Bedford/St. Martin's; and Leasa Burton, publisher, for helping us think through different iterations of this project since 2004. Leasa's kind editorial mentorship helped us to conceptualize (and reconceptualize) our project from initial proposal to finished product. We also offer our gratitude to Sophia Snyder, editor, for her insight, attention to detail, and unending patience. At every turn, she proved herself to be a remarkably attentive and fun editor to work with, coaxing us toward deadlines, listening patiently to our (ok, Cheryl's) rants, clarifying our approach, and ensuring that this book would be relevant to the many audiences we wanted to reach. Plus, there's nothing better than bonding with your editor over lolcats.

We'd also like to recognize the many other people at Bedford who contributed to this book: Laura Clark, production editor, for her patience and attention to detail that included assuring us a last-minute change to correctly reference a musical instrument in Chapter 3 would be fixed well after page proofs were due; Rachel Childs, editorial assistant, for any number of behind-the-scenes tasks; Arthur Johnson, copy editor, who showed us the kinds of conversations good copyediting can prompt between authors, developmental editors, and production editors; Marine Miller, cover designer, who diligently worked to design a book cover about design for authors who are designers, never an easy feat; Molly Parke, executive marketing manager, and Karita dos Santos, market development manager, for working to get the word out about the book; Martha Friedman, photo research manager, and Rona Tuccillo, art researcher, for dealing valiantly with hard-to-find rights holders and complicated multimedia permissions; and Jake Kawatski, indexer, for his careful attention to themes and subjects. Thank you, thank you, thank you.

Thanks are also due to the following reviewers for their invaluable feedback on early drafts of our manuscript: Sarah Arroyo, California State University

Long Beach; Florence Bacabac, Dixie State College of Utah; Lisa Bickmore, Salt Lake City Community College; Russell Carpenter, Eastern Kentucky University; Angela Crow, James Madison University; John Eliason, Gonzaga University; Mary Isbell, University of Connecticut–Storrs; Justin Jory, University of Colorado–Colorado Springs; Daniel Keller, Ohio State University; Marshall Kitchens, Oakland University; Ben Lauren, Florida International University; Alex Layne, Purdue University; Candice Melzow, Texas A&M University; Jennifer Nish, University of Kansas; Jill Parrott, Eastern Kentucky University; Erin Presley, Eastern Kentucky University; Jenny Rice, University of Kentucky; Eileen Seifert, DePaul University; and Katherine Tirabassi, Keene State College. Their insights helped us to focus our approach and to keep the needs of a diverse instructor and student population in mind as we wrote.

Finally, we'd like to say a special thanks to the people in our immediate lives who have supported our work on this project. We are grateful to our many students and friends who read through drafts, tested early chapters, and allowed us to use examples of their work to help others learn. These samples would not have been possible without their graciousness. We also appreciate the mentorship and guidance we received from faculty at Michigan Technological University during our doctoral program and thank them for supporting our interests in multimodal rhetorics and literacies. Finally, our work on this book was made possible with the support and friendship of colleagues at our respective institutions, Washington State University, New Mexico State University, and Illinois State University.

Kristin gives thanks to her co-writers, Jenny and Cheryl, for their friendship, collaboration, and mentorship from the graduate school years through the tenure process. She would also like to thank her amazing colleagues and graduate students at Washington State University. Watching Dr. Patricia Ericsson gracefully integrate multimodality into their first-year composition course, and then seeing talented instructors creatively and critically engage with a multimodal pedagogy, she believes has been an invaluable and awe-inspiring experience. Thanks to all of her past undergraduate students who make her job worth doing, especially those who gave permission for their work to be used in this book—Courteney Dowd, Ariel Popp, Nicholas Winters, and Elyse Canfield. Thanks to those family members, friends, and friends of friends who graciously share their artistic talents with the world, and allowed her to share a piece of that in this book—Matt Seigel, Elena Duff, *Pank*, Jeff Kuure, Adam Arola, Leigh Feldman, and Tom O'Toole. And finally, thanks to Jeff, who continues to feed her heart, soul, and belly with all things good.

Jenny would like to extend her thanks to her partner, Kathryn, who graciously took on extra childcare and household duties while she worked on the book. Her overall support and willingness to talk through ideas were instrumental in the project's completion. Jenny would also like to thank Edgar Barrantes, CC Chamberlin, and Phillip Johnson for their permission to reproduce several of the examples used in the book, as well as the many students with whom she has worked over the years. She has learned an immeasurable amount about multi-modal composing from their efforts and experiences.

Cheryl would like to thank all of her students in her multimodal composition classes over the years for helping her to better understand how to teach the kinds of projects this book outlines. In particular, she thanks her Fall 2011 class at Illinois State University, which user-tested early chapters and provided excellent feedback on how to keep or improve sections. A big thanks also goes to graduate students Jason Dockter and Barbi Smyser-Fauble for graciously user-testing the near-completed book in their composition classes and providing their syllabi for the Instructor's Manual. To Tara Reeser, who taught her what it means to *really* be a professional in publishing, to merge the multiple lives of editors and publishers in and out of the classroom, and to remember that great ideas can come to fruition under the right circumstances, she promises to never cease learning. Without the generous, scholarly, and pedagogical support of her besty colleagues Laura Erskine and Shamira Gelbman—who helped spark the idea that this book should be for teachers across the curriculum as much as for those in writing studies, and who read many drafts of chapters during writing group meetings at the CoffeeHound—this book would not have come together in the way it did. She will be forever grateful to Joan Mullin, who prepared so many delightful meals over which deep and grounded thoughts about multi-modal composing could be hashed out; Joan is an extraordinary mentor and the best role model a strong woman could ever want. Colleagues and friends Tasha Dunn and Chrissy Cataldo provided much-needed comic relief and kittehs throughout the process, and Susana Rodriguez took remarkable photos of her two fat cats, Beau and Regine, which were used in the book for additional comic relief. She owes a big hug and many odd days out doing barn tours with these ladies. Thank you! And, of course, without being true and loyal friends, Cheryl, Kristin, and Jenny could have never gotten through the process of writing collaboratively. It was a test and testament to their understanding of each other, and this book is all the better because of them.

Digital and Print Resources for *Writer/Designer*

Writer/Designer doesn't stop with this book. You'll find both free and affordable premium digital resources to help students get even more out of the book and your course, as well as package options that can save your students money. You'll also find convenient instructor resources. To learn more about or to order any of the products below, contact your Bedford/St. Martin's sales representative, email sales support (sales_support@bfwpub.com), or visit the Web site at **bedfordstmartins.com/writerdesigner/catalog**.

Let Students Choose Their Format

Bedford/St. Martin's e-books let students do more and pay less. Students can purchase *Writer/Designer* in e-book formats for computers, tablets, and e-readers. Now instructors can customize our downloadable e-books by adding their own content or removing chapters so that students pay less for a shorter book. For more details, visit **bedfordstmartins.com/writerdesigner/formats**.

Package and Save

Add more value to your course by packaging a handbook or reader with *Writer/ Designer*—and save 20%. To learn more about package options or any of the products below, contact your Bedford/St. Martin's sales representative or visit the Web site at **bedfordstmartins.com/writerdesigner/catalog**.

- *Writer's Help*, **by Diana Hacker, Stephen A. Bernhardt, and Nancy Sommers**, rethinks where a handbook lives and how it works. It responds to searches by students who may—or may not—know standard composition terminology. To order *Writer's Help* packaged with *Writer/Designer*, use **ISBN 978-1-4576-7694-9**.

- *EasyWriter*, **Fifth Edition, by Andrea Lunsford**, distills Lunsford's teaching and research into the essentials that today's writers need to make good choices in any rhetorical situation. To order *EasyWriter* packaged with *Writer/Designer*, use **ISBN 978-1-4576-7692-5**.

- *A Pocket Style Manual*, **Sixth Edition, by Diana Hacker and Nancy Sommers**, is a straightforward, inexpensive quick reference, whose flexible content, slim format, and brief length make it easy for students to keep it with them for every assignment, in any class. To order *A Pocket Style Manual* packaged with *Writer/Designer*, use **ISBN 978-1-4576-7693-2**.

Try *Re:Writing 2* for the Fun of It

What's the fun of teaching writing if you can't try something new? The best collection of open writing resources on the Web, *Re:Writing 2* gives you and your students even more ways to think, watch, practice, and learn about writing concepts. Listen to Nancy Sommers on using a teacher's comments to revise. Try a logic puzzle. Consult our resources for writing centers. Because free stuff is fun: **bedfordstmartins.com/rewriting**.

Instructor Resources

bedfordstmartins.com/writerdesigner/catalog

You have a lot to do in your course. Bedford/St. Martin's wants to make it easy for you to find the support you need—and to get it quickly.

The ***Instructor's Manual for Writer/Designer*** is available as a PDF that can be downloaded from the Bedford/St. Martin's online catalog. In addition to chapter overviews and teaching tips, the Instructor's Manual includes sample syllabi, an annotated bibliography, and suggestions for assessing multimodal work.

Free **Bedford Coursepacks** allow you to easily integrate our most popular content into your own course management systems. For details, visit **bedfordstmartins.com/coursepacks**.

TeachingCentral (**bedfordstmartins.com/teachingcentral**) offers the entire list of Bedford/St. Martin's print and online professional resources in one place. You'll find landmark reference works, sourcebooks on pedagogical issues, award-winning collections, and practical advice for the classroom—all free for instructors.

Bits: Ideas for Teaching Composition (**bedfordbits.com**) collects creative ideas for teaching a range of composition topics in an easily searchable blog format. A community of teachers—leading scholars, authors, and editors—discuss revision, research, grammar and style, technology, peer review, and much more. Take, use, adapt, and pass the ideas around. Then come back to the site to comment or share your own suggestions.

Contents

:e: For readings that go beyond the printed page, see bedfordstmartins.com/writerdesigner.

2 | Analyzing Multimodal Projects   20

3 | Choosing a Genre and Pitching Your Project 40

4 | Working with Multimodal Sources 57

:e: bedfordstmartins.com/writerdesigner

Introduction for Students

Although the three of us are trained as writing teachers, we have always been interested in new media and nontextual means of communicating. Don't get us wrong; we love words, and we love helping people learn how to craft them. Writing will continue to be important for a long time to come. However, we've also come to see that elements beyond words can be just as—or more!—effective in conveying a message. Our goal in this book is to help you take advantage of every possibility that's out there—not just words but also sound, images, movement, and more—so you can create communications that perfectly meet your goals, your situation, and the needs of your audience.

We often ask our students to create texts of all kinds, and we decided to write this book as a way to support writers in that complex and sometimes messy process. As writers, designers, and communicators who for many years have worked on creating interactive Flash projects, video presentations, Web sites, social networking profiles, new media journals, and more, we are interested in conveying information and ideas using the most appropriate means and media at our disposal. Through this book, you'll learn from the successes we've had and the mistakes we've made as teachers and authors.

Notice we just said "authors" here, but elsewhere in this book we'll refer to the people who produce content as "designers," "writers," and "communicators." You might be saying that writers don't design, or that communicators don't write. We don't believe that's true (and that's why we called this book *Writer/ Designer*). Using a multimodal approach to reading or composing a text, you'll start to recognize that *all* writing is designed, even if it doesn't look like much thought was put into those one-inch margins. And the converse is usually true as well, in that most designs involve some kind of writing. We believe that communication comes in many forms and that it is all created with some deliberate attention to writing and design. It may not be a kind of writing that you recognize or that you think would "count" as acceptable writing in a professional setting such as school or work, but as this book will show you, even something as seemingly simple as a text message can be carefully written and designed.

At this point in your life, you've likely come to realize that good writing doesn't just happen. You're probably familiar with the idea that writing is a process, with various stages required to get to a final product. Similarly, good multimodal projects don't just happen—they involve planning, researching, drafting, and revising. Although these stages may look a little different for each writer and each project, being able to draw on this basic process can help you create texts that will be complete and persuasive to your intended audience. This book will help you hone a composing process that works for you, no matter what kind of project you are creating.

Just as important, this book will provide you with a toolkit for analyzing and creating texts in many modes and for many different audiences. Although we'll talk a lot about digital texts, we'll provide ideas for nondigital texts, too. Also, this isn't a how-to book about specific technologies or software applications. We'll give you guidance on how to think through the *who*, *what*, *why*, and *how* of your projects so that you can use whichever communication mode, genre, or technology will best suit your audience and purpose. You'll find that this approach is more beneficial in the long run since you'll be able to apply these practices to whatever new technology emerges next.

Features of the Book and How to Use Them

We spent a lot of time thinking about how to design this book to support the variety of projects you might take on. We've worked to provide clear explanations and lots of examples, particularly in the Case Studies, to help illustrate the concepts and practices we talk about. We have included short Process! activities throughout each chapter so that you can get some quick experience putting concepts into practice. We've also included longer Write/Design assignments in every chapter to guide you through the steps of creating larger-scale projects. Finally, we have embedded e-Pages links to digital, interactive material that furthers the learning in each chapter. **e** This icon, which you will find throughout the book, lets you know that there is e-Pages content available, including multimedia content we can't represent in print. We have used all of these activities and assignments with our own students to help them develop ideas, design projects, and communicate through multiple modes. We don't like busywork, so each Process! activity and Write/Design assignment was set up specifically to help you understand concepts and move your project toward completion.

Above all, as you use this book, we want you to keep in mind that creating multimodal projects can be a lot of fun. Yes, there are bound to be frustrations along the way as you work through the many possibilities, but your communication options are no longer limited to typing words in a twelve-point font on an 8.5″ x 11″ piece of paper. We invite you to dive in, experiment, and see what opportunities you have to convey your ideas, arguments, and information.

Writer/Designer

A Guide to Making Multimodal Projects

What Are Multimodal Projects?

Academic essays, biology posters, statistical PowerPoint presentations, lolcats . . . what do all of these texts have in common? They are all **multimodal**.

The word *multimodal* is a mash-up of *multiple* and *mode*. A *mode* is a way of communicating, such as the words we're using to explain our ideas in this paragraph or the images we use throughout this book to illustrate various concepts. *Multimodal* describes how we combine multiple different ways of communicating in everyday life.

For instance, lolcats, a well-known Internet meme, are multimodal. They combine photographs of cats with words written in humorously incorrect grammar to create a text that uses both visuals and language—*multiple modes*—to be funny.

You might be saying to yourself, "Wait, is a lolcat really a text?" Yes. **Text** traditionally means written words. But because we want to talk about the visuals, sounds, and movement that make up multimedia, we use the term *text* to refer to a piece of communication as a whole. A text can be anything from a lolcat to a concert tee shirt to a dictionary to a performance.

Figure 1.1 Lolcats Are Multimodal

This book will give you the multimodal tools to do it right!

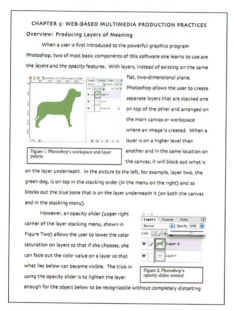

CHAPTER 5: WEB-BASED MULTIMEDIA PRODUCTION PRACTICES

Overview: Producing Layers of Meaning

When a user is first introduced to the powerful graphics program Photoshop, two of most basic components of this software one learns to use are the *layers* and the *opacity* features. With layers, instead of existing on the same flat, two-dimensional plane, Photoshop allows the user to create separate layers that are stacked one on top of the other and arranged on the main canvas or workspace where an image is created. When a layer is on a higher level than another and in the same location on the canvas, it will block out what is on the layer underneath. In the picture to the left, for example, layer two, the green dog, is on top in the stacking order (in the menu on the right) and so blocks out the blue bone that is on the layer underneath it (on both the canvas and in the stacking menu).

However, an opacity slider (upper right corner of the layer stacking menu, shown in Figure Two) allows the user to lower the color saturation on layers so that if she chooses, she can fade out the color value on a layer so that what lies below can become visible. The trick in using the opacity slider is to lighten the layer enough for the object below to be recognizable without completely distorting

Figure 1.2 A Dissertation Is a Multimodal Text

Figure 1.3 A Performance Is a Multimodal Text

Figure 1.4 A Web Site Is a Multimodal Text

Writers choose modes of communication for every text they create. For example, the author of a lolcat chooses the cat photo (usually based on what is happening in the photo and whether that action might make for a good caption) and decides where to place the caption on the photo and what color and typeface to use for the caption. Sometimes these choices are unconscious, like when an author uses Microsoft Word's default typeface and margins when writing a paper for class. To produce a successful text, writers must be able to consciously use different modes both alone and in combination with each other to communicate their ideas to others.

The Modes: How Do They Work?

All kinds of texts are multimodal: newspapers, science reports, advertisements, billboards, scrapbooks, music videos—the list is endless. Consider, for example, all of the modes at play in a simple TV

Are All Texts Multimodal?

We said that multimodal texts are made up of multiple ways of communicating; for example, a multimodal text such as a lolcat might combine words and pictures to make meaning. So what about something like a research paper, which is mostly words? Is that a multimodal text?

The answer is yes! Let's take **Figure 1.2** as an example. It might seem that an audience could understand this text's argument just by reading the written words. In fact, to understand the full message being communicated in the text, the audience has to make sense of other elements as well. They must also look at the images and read the captions that explain what the images contain. The format of the text—a single column of black printed words on a white background, with a margin on either side—also tells the audience something important: that this text is probably an academic work of some kind. (In fact, it's a page from Jenny's dissertation.) Knowing what kind of text it is will influence the way the audience reads it.

Figure 1.5 *ix: visualizing composition: Text*

What are multimodal texts and how do they function? Work through this interactive discussion of *text* using multimodal principles. Visit **bedfordstmartins.com/writerdesigner** to complete this tutorial.

Are All Multimodal Texts Digital?

Multimodal texts don't have to be digital. The dissertation in **Figure 1.2** was created on a computer but then was printed and bound into a book copy for the library. No matter whether a text is created on a computer, on paper, or in some other technology, writer/designers can still use the multiple combinations of words, photos, color, layout, and more to communicate their information.

commercial—there usually is music, the voice of an announcer, video showing the product, text on the screen giving you a price or a Web address, and often much more. Each of these modes plays a role in the advertiser's argument for why you should buy its product. The music is selected to give the product a certain feel (young and hip, perhaps, or safe and reliable). The gender of the announcer and the tone, volume, and other qualities of his or her voice reflect whom the advertiser is trying to reach. The choice of whether to use video or animation, color or black and white, slow motion or other special effects, are all deliberate *modal* considerations based on what the advertiser is trying to sell and to whom. Although each mode plays a role in the overall message, it is the combination of modes—the *multi*modality—that creates the full piece of communication.

To help you think through the different modes that may be present in a multimodal text, we're going to introduce you to five terms from the work of the New London Group, a collection of education and literacy scholars who first promoted the concept of multimodal literacies. They outlined five modes of communication—linguistic, visual, aural, gestural, and spatial—which they found could be

Figure 1.6 The Five Modes of Communication

This chart of the modes is based on a diagram created by the New London Group.

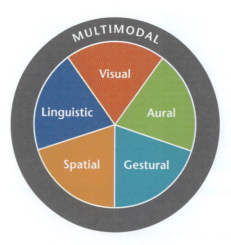

applied to all texts. The next section will help you better understand how these individual modes work.

Linguistic Mode

The linguistic mode refers to the use of language, which usually means written or spoken words. When we think about the ways the linguistic mode is used to make or understand meaning, we can consider:

- word choice
- the delivery of spoken or written text
- the organization of writing or speech into phrases, sentences, paragraphs, etc.
- the development and coherence of individual words and ideas

While these aren't the only possibilities for understanding how the linguistic mode works, this list gives you a starting place from which to consider how words and language function. And although we've listed it first—and though it's the mode you probably have the most practice with—the linguistic mode is not always the most important mode of communication. (Whether it is or not depends on what other modes are at play in a text, what kind of text it is, and many other factors.)

The linguistic mode and the ability to use it carefully matter very much in contemporary communication. For example, consider a widely criticized comment made by Carl-Henric Svanberg, chairman of the global oil company BP, following the 2010 oil spill in the Gulf of Mexico. After meeting with President Obama, Svanberg announced that his company was committed to the cleanup and stated that BP "care[s] about the small people." Although he likely was referring to BP's commitment to helping individual citizens, his choice of words—"small people"—infuriated the public because it demeaned those impacted by the spill and implied that the disruption to their lives was not of great concern.

Process! In 2011, Danielle E. Sucher created an extension for the Chrome Web browser called Jailbreak the Patriarchy, to wildly mixed reviews. This extension "genderswaps" all pronouns and gendered words, replacing "him" with "her," "mother" with "father," and so on. Try making this switch yourself by rewriting the linguistic content on your favorite Web site (or run a Web search for the add-on and install it). What linguistic choices do you notice? Are there any word choices or phrasings that you feel are particularly effective or ineffective? If so, which ones and why? How does genderswapping pronouns make you feel? What are some possible critiques of such a switch?

Visual Mode

The visual mode refers to the use of images and other characteristics that readers see. Billboards, flyers, television, Web sites, lighted advertising displays, even grocery store shelves bombard us with visual information in an effort to attract our attention. We can use this mode to communicate representations of how something looks or how someone is feeling, to instruct, to persuade, and to entertain, among other things. The visual mode includes:

- color
- layout
- style
- size
- perspective

These Twitter profiles (**Figs. 1.7 and 1.8**) have a lot of words (the linguistic mode), but their visual mode—the colors, layout, profile pictures, and logo—plays a big role in how users read and understand each page.

Figure 1.7 Kristin Arola's Twitter Feed

Figure 1.8 Jenny Sheppard's Twitter Feed

Process! Look closely at the visual mode in the Twitter profiles shown in **Figures 1.7 and 1.8**, or go online to check out two of your friends' Twitter profiles. What visual differences do you see between the profiles? Do these differences shape your understanding of the person behind each profile? What do you assume he/she is like? What do you assume he/she uses Twitter for? Do you have a Twitter profile? What visual template did you choose, and why?

Aural Mode

The aural mode focuses on sound. Whether we are talking about a speech, a video demonstration, sound effects on a Web site, or the audio elements of a radio program, the aural mode provides multiple ways of communicating and understanding a message, including:

- music
- sound effects
- ambient noise/sounds
- silence
- tone of voice in spoken language
- volume of sound
- emphasis and accent

Although most of us are used to hearing sound all around us every day, we don't often pay attention to how it signals information, including feelings, responses, or needed actions. It's easy to conceive how a spoken message communicates, but what about the increasingly tense background music in a TV drama, or the sounds that let us know when a computer is starting up? Whether big or small, each of these aural components conveys meaning. The opening theme song for *The Colbert Report*—a satirical news program on Comedy Central—famously ends with the screech of a bald eagle, but this eagle isn't the patriotic, feel-good symbol that the bald eagle is typically presented as in the United States. This ironic usage of the eagle supports the comedic tone of the program, in which Colbert pretends to be a conservative pundit.

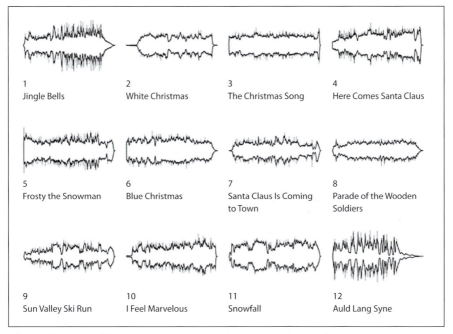

Figure 1.9 Graphic Comparison of Christmas Song Waveforms

Audio can also have visual aspects, as these representations show.

Watch this short video. What aural modal elements do you hear? What effect do these have on the tone of the piece? How would the tone of the video change if a country or bluegrass song were playing in the background? Visit **bedfordstmartins.com /writerdesigner** to watch this video.

Process!

Figure 1.10 *Wanna Work Together?* by Creative Commons

Spatial Mode

The spatial mode is about physical arrangement. This can include how a brochure opens and the way it leads a reader through the text. For example, see the brochure in **Figure 1.11**. The designer created this conference program so that each fold is slightly smaller than the one below it, allowing readers to have a tab for each day of presentations. The spatial mode can also refer to the placement of navigation on a Web page to maximize access for users. This mode helps us to understand why physical spaces such as grocery stores or classrooms are arranged in particular ways to encourage certain kinds of behavior (such as all chairs in a classroom facing toward the center of the room to encourage discussion and collaboration). The spatial mode includes:

- arrangement
- organization
- proximity between people or objects

Attention to the spatial mode has become increasingly important as we create content for and interact within online environments. The author of a text must pay attention to how his or her content is organized so that readers can find their way through the text without difficulty.

Figure 1.11 Tabbed Brochure Utilizing the Spatial Mode

Figure 1.12 Cheryl Ball's Twitter Feed

The designers of Twitter chose how to lay out the basic profile page (with the tweets in the right column and info about the user on the left), and users can choose design templates and profile images—all of which means that *layout* draws on spatial, visual, and linguistic modes of communication, showing that it's nearly impossible for a text *not* to use multiple modes at once.

Visit the home page for your favorite retail, entertainment, or news Web site. Notice how the spatial mode is used: Where is your eye drawn? How are the elements on the page laid out? What effect does this spatial arrangement have on how you read, use, and understand the information on the page? How would your interaction with the page be different if, say, the information found at the top of the page were suddenly swapped with the information at the bottom?

Process!

Gestural Mode

The gestural mode refers to the way movement, such as body language, can make meaning. When we interact with people in real life or watch them on-screen, we can tell a lot about how they are feeling and what they are trying to communicate. The gestural mode includes:

- facial expressions
- hand gestures
- body language
- interaction between people

The gestural has always been important in face-to-face conversations and in the theater, but understanding the gestural mode is just as

Figure 1.13 Katie Couric's Opening to Her First Newscast

Figure 1.14 Brian Williams's Opening to His Newscast

important when communication takes place through virtual interactions on-screen. Whether we are participating in a videoconference with colleagues, a gaming raid with friends, or an online chat with family, the gestural mode provides an important way of connecting (or showing an inability to connect) to other people.

Consider, for example, how Katie Couric opened her first CBS newscast standing alongside her desk, and contrast it with Brian Williams's stiff and formal posture behind his desk during his newscast (**Figs. 1.13 and 1.14**). Couric's body position was an attempt to be more approachable than other anchors, but her more personable gestures translated to more gender-stereotyped ideas of femininity, which worked against Couric, the first female solo anchor on a prime-time broadcast network newscast.

Visit **bedfordstmartins.com/writerdesigner** to watch this video of President Obama delivering his second inaugural address. Notice how the president uses the gestural mode to support his points. Pay particular attention to his hand gestures and facial expressions. Do you find his use of the gestural mode effective? Why or why not?

Process!

Compare the video of President Obama with a video of Condoleezza Rice, US secretary of state under George W. Bush, giving a speech at the Republican National Convention in 2012. How do Obama's and Rice's gestures differ?

Figure 1.15
President Obama Speaking

Figure 1.16
Condoleezza Rice Speaking

Composing for Access

One cool thing about multimodality is that it can attend to multiple senses, which is sometimes necessary if a reader has a preference or need for one mode of communication over another. When creating multimodal texts, authors should *always* remember that not every reader will be exactly like them, either in culture, society, class, race, gender, or ability. A text should be composed so that readers with limited vision, hearing, or touch—among other possible differences within an audience—can still interact with the text. For instance, imagine that you're filming someone who speaks American Sign Language—would you film the person from the shoulders up, cutting their hands from the shot? No! As you analyze and compose multimodal texts, be careful to compose for as many different users with as many different backgrounds and abilities as possible.

Understanding Media and Affordances

Let's say you want to share how much you adore your dog because your dog is so cute! You have hundreds of photos. These pictures are your *media* (singular *medium*) that you could share. The *medium* is the way in which your text reaches your audience. Other media you might use are video, speech, or paper (not a research paper per se, but the physical artifact on which a research paper would be printed).

Different media use different combinations of modes and are good at doing different things. We've all heard the expression "a picture is worth a thousand words." Sometimes it is much easier and more effective to use an image to show someone how to do something or how you are feeling. Say, for example, that the reason you wanted a picture of your dog is to show your friend in another state what the dog looks like (see **Fig. 1.17**). A picture will quickly convey more information in this situation than will a written description.

Figure 1.17 Poor, Sad, Adorable Enid

At other times, words may work better than images when we are trying to explain an idea because words can be more descriptive and to the point. It may take too many pictures to convey the same idea quickly (see **Fig. 1.18**).

> **Enid wakes me up at 4am on the day I'm leaving. Lies on my chest and stares at me. 22 hours later I get to my hotel.** — in Saint Louis, MO.

Figure 1.18 Facebook Status Update Contextualizing Enid's Pitiful Look

And in other situations in which we are trying to communicate how something should be done, it can be more useful to create an animation or video that demonstrates the steps in a process than to write out instructions.

These different strengths and weaknesses of media (video, writing, pictures, etc.) and modes are called *affordances*. The visual mode *affords* us the opportunity to communicate emotion in an immediate way, while the linguistic mode *affords* us the time we need to communicate a set of detailed steps. Writer/designers think through the affordances of the modes and media available before choosing the right text for the right situation. Keep in mind that modal affordances largely depend on how the mode is used and in what context. In other words, the strengths and weaknesses of each mode are dependent on, and influenced by, the ways in which the modes are combined, in what media, and to what ends.

CASE STUDY

Modes, Media, and Affordances

Although we've given you examples in this chapter of how each mode works on its own to communicate, we want to finish this chapter with an extended example of how all of the modes work together in a single multimodal text. Throughout this example, we're going to highlight some of the key concepts we want you to pay attention to.

The documents in **Figures 1.19 and 1.20** were created by the US government to communicate information about nationwide economic recovery efforts. In the 1930s, the United States was suffering through a severe economic meltdown, known now as the Great Depression. To help alleviate the situation, President Franklin Delano Roosevelt (FDR) created the Works Progress Administration, which put millions of Americans to work repairing and updating the United States' infrastructure, including building highways and fixing streets. The map in **Figure 1.19** shows a state-by-state and county-by-county textual and visual overview of street projects funded by the government.

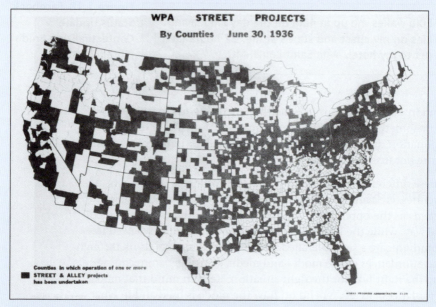

Figure 1.19 Map of WPA Street Projects, 1936

This map, printed in the 1930s as part of the Works Progress Administration government recovery program, is a multimodal text.

The words on this map (the **linguistic mode**) describe what we are looking at. The shaded areas on the map visually represent locations where at least one project had taken place. Here, the color-coding (the **visual mode**) shows us what areas received the most assistance. The information is organized in map form (the **spatial mode**), which positions the color-coded points according to US counties. The visual and spatial modes work together to help us make comparisons between locations. For example, the densely shaded area in the Northeast, where the US population was most concentrated at the time, can be compared against the relatively barren spots in the West, where fewer people lived. A spatial representation of the states from 1936, when there were only forty-eight states, will be different from an 1803 map that focuses on the Louisiana Purchase, or from a 2011 map showing all fifty states. So in this map, the linguistic, visual, and spatial modes work together to show readers where street projects occurred in 1936.

Now consider how this map could have been read differently if the proportion of words and numbers (linguistic mode) to visual and spatial information had been changed to favor the linguistic elements. For instance, what if, instead of the street projects map, readers only got large tables of data for each state, county, or project? (In fact, other parts of the WPA report from which the map is taken do include many data tables, such as the one seen in **Figure 1.20**.) The linguistic mode often affords readers specificity, exactness, and logical connections, but this can slow readers down as they work to make sense of the information. The visual mode, on the other hand, often can't be as detailed. We don't know from the map, for example, *how many* projects were completed in each area. But a visual presentation of complex information can allow readers to make quick comparisons. This ability for quick comparison is an affordance of the visual mode, particularly within the particular medium of the printed map.

We should also consider the affordances of the **media** available at the time of distribution. In 1936, radio and print (typically government reports or newspapers) would have been the primary media used to communicate to the public.

VALUE OF MATERIALS, SUPPLIES AND EQUIPMENT PROCURED FOR WPA PROJECTS, BY TYPES OF PROJECTS Through May 30, 1936		
Type of Project	Total Value	
	Amount	Percent
TOTAL	$ 142,935,931	100.0
Highways, roads, and streets	45,952,629	32.1
Public buildings	27,297,802	19.1
Housing	67,172	0.1
Parks and playgrounds	20,601,596	14.4
Flood control and other conservation	6,817,343	4.8
Water supply and sewer systems	24,065,084	16.8
Electric utilities	586,279	0.4
Transportation	4,156,418	2.9
Educational, professional and clerical	2,944,215	2.1
Goods	3,822,563	2.7
Sanitation and health	3,287,372	2.3
Miscellaneous	3,337,458	2.3

Figure 1.20 Table of WPA Projects Data, 1936

A data table from a 1936 report showing the value of materials used in WPA projects.

Printing in color would have been prohibitively expensive, so black-and-white visuals and written text had to be used. In **Figure 1.21** we can see a more modern version of a similar report, a digitally based map from the Recovery.gov Web site illustrating economic recovery in the United States in 2009–2010. As FDR did in establishing the Works Progress Administration, President Obama created the American Recovery and Reinvestment Act to stimulate job creation and repairs to the US infrastructure during difficult economic times.

Figure 1.21 is a contemporary version of the 1936 WPA report; it appears on a Web site and is interactive (as the highlighting and pop-up about New Mexico show). Its medium is a Web-based map as opposed to a print-based map. It uses linguistic, visual, and spatial modes of communication, just like the 1936 map does, but it also includes interactivity (a gestural mode). Below the map, there is an interactive search tool to find specific funding information by zip code. Because of the affordances of the Web (such as cheaper use of multiple colors and the use of electronic databases and interactivity), this map communicates

Figure 1.21 An Interactive Map from the Recovery.gov Web Site

a lot more information than a printed map in 1936 would have been able to communicate. These differences don't mean that the Web is a better medium than print—just that, due to the technological changes in the last century, the Web allows for more complex and detailed information to be conveyed using a similarly sized map.

Writing/Designing Multimodally

The image in **Figure 1.21** highlights at least four different modes of communication being used in one text (linguistic, spatial, gestural, visual). Other texts, such as video interviews on the Recovery.gov Web site, combine all *five* modes, including the aural. One way to think about the different modes of communication is as a set of tools. You may not use all of them for a single project, because each mode has its own strengths and weaknesses in specific situations—just as a wrench is more useful in fixing a faucet than a hammer is. Like the tools in a toolbox, though, modes can sometimes be used in ways that weren't intended but that get the job done just as well (like a screwdriver being used to pry open a can of paint).

Together, the many modes that make up texts are useful in different situations. Multimodality gives writers additional tools for designing effective texts. This is particularly true when writers are trying to create a single text that will appeal to the interests of a large and diverse group of readers. By understanding who their readers are, what they need to know, and how they will use the information, authors can create texts that satisfy a specific rhetorical situation, a concept we will cover in Chapter 2.

write/design assignment

Describing Multimodality in Everyday Texts

To get a better sense of how prevalent multimodality is in all texts, spend the next few days collecting examples of multimodal texts as you go about your daily schedule. Maybe you can keep a blog where you upload, link to, or describe these texts, or you could start a Twitter hashtag where you briefly describe what modes the texts use. Count the number of texts that use all five modes of communication (linguistic, aural, visual, spatial, gestural), and see what patterns you can discover across the texts. Are they similar types of texts? Do they come from a similar time period or location or publication? Which two texts are the most different from each other? How are the modes used in those texts, and does that contribute to how different they are?

2 Analyzing Multimodal Projects

Have you ever been walking through town, and one flyer among the hundreds of flyers you see every day stands out so much that you can't help but stop and read it? Have you ever been rushing to leave the house when your favorite song starts playing on the radio, and you have to listen to it before you can leave? Have you ever found a Web site link or online video so exciting or funny that you have to immediately share it with your Facebook friends? These multimodal texts are captivating—they capture your attention and encourage you to interact with them and share them. Chances are the multimodal texts that caught and held your attention are the ones that used the most effective design choices. These are the kinds of texts we want you to build. In this chapter you will learn how to analyze multimodal texts to discover how effective design choices are made for different texts in different situations.

Writer/designers have a wide variety of options for creating an effective text. What makes a text effective depends on a number of factors: What is the author's reason for creating the text? What audience is the author trying to reach? In what place, time, or situation is the text being created? Analyzing these factors will help you understand the projects of other writer/designers and will help you create your own multimodal texts (a task we'll take on in Chapter 3).

Figure 2.1 An Effective Multimodal Flyer

This flyer on a school bulletin board caught Cheryl's attention. It was printed in color and in landscape orientation on 11″ x 17″ paper.

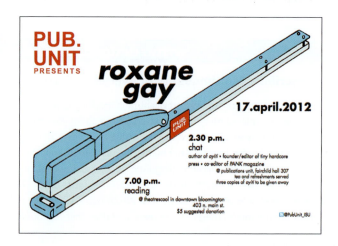

Rhetoric and Multimodality

When we talk about "effective" or "successful" texts, we're talking about rhetoric. Texts need to be created for a purpose, to persuade an audience toward change in some way; **rhetoric** is the study of making texts that effectively persuade an audience toward change. Echoing that old philosophical question—if a tree falls in the forest and no one is around to hear it, does it make a sound?—if a text doesn't induce change, then it isn't rhetorically successful. *Successful* multimodal persuasion is what this book is about.

You're probably familiar with some forms of persuading others to take action in favor of an author's viewpoint, such as when an advertisement tries to persuade us to choose a particular political candidate, a new summer outfit, a different brand of toothpaste, a recycling option, or a party to attend. Sometimes this change is more subtle and the action is less explicit, such as when we read a novel to better understand the human condition (or simply to relax), or—as in the Recovery.gov example in the previous chapter—when we explore a government Web site to learn more about how our taxes are spent and who they benefit.

As readers, we can choose whether to act based on how effectively a text persuades us. Let's think about a musical example. While a musician probably has many hopes for a song—that it speaks to people and is artistically meaningful, for example—one hope is that listeners will enjoy the song enough to purchase it. Whether listeners buy it depends on a lot of things: whether they like the song's lyrics, whether the song speaks to them in some way, whether they have the money, what format the song is available in, what technology they have for listening to the song, etc. The song's author had to think through all of these possibilities when creating and distributing the song. In the end, the author has created a text that asks readers to make a choice. A particular listener's choice may be to do nothing (not to listen to or buy the song), but that's still a choice.

Our reactions typically depend on how well an author is able to address the **rhetorical situation**. The rhetorical situation is the set of circumstances in which an author creates a text. Authors have to pay attention to four factors: their intended **audience**, their **purpose** for communicating, the **context** in which their text will be read, and the **genre** they choose for their text if they want to be effective communicators.

Rhetorical Analysis

Understanding the situation in which an author composed a text can help us better understand a text's meaning and make judgments about its effectiveness. Who was the author? Why did he or she compose this text? When and where was it composed? Whom did the author want to reach? Why is the text in this particular form? Thinking through the rhetorical situation like this is called rhetorical analysis. A **rhetorical analysis** is a method of describing the context in which an author wants to communicate his or her purpose or call for action to the intended audience in a genre. Below, we offer the five areas to address—audience, purpose, context, author, and genre—and offer some questions to consider when performing a rhetorical analysis.

Figure 2.2 A Parody Video for Rhetorical Analysis

Cheryl decided to parody (right) Psy's "Gangnam Style" video (**genre**, left) for her friend's (**audience**) birthday (**context**) because her friend's last name sounds similar to *Gangnam* (**purpose**).

Audience

The audience is the intended readership for a text. There may be more than one intended audience, and there may also be more than one actual audience. Consider a pop-country song playing over the sound system at a mall. The songwriter's intended audience is likely pop-country fans, and her secondary audience may be country or pop-music fans. Yet, in this context, the actual audience is anyone who happens to hear it.

In a rhetorical analysis, your job is to pay attention to the intended primary and secondary audiences. While it is not necessarily your job to consider how the text will function if read by those outside the intended audience, doing so can sometimes be illuminating.

When analyzing audience, consider these questions:

- Who is the intended audience?
- Who might be the secondary audience(s)?
- What values or opinions do the primary and secondary audiences hold? Does the author appeal to these values or opinions in any way?

Figure 2.3 *ix: visualizing composition: Audience*

Work through this interactive discussion for more practice with *audience*. Visit **bedfordstmartins .com/writerdesigner** to complete this tutorial.

Purpose

Describing a text's purpose may sound somewhat simplistic, yet it is important to consider a range of possible intentions—while there may be a large-scale purpose, there often are also secondary purposes. For example, a billboard for a local steakhouse has the primary purpose of attracting new clientele, but it may have the secondary purpose of solidifying existing customers' opinion of the restaurant as a fun-loving family establishment.

When analyzing purpose, consider these questions:

- What do you consider to be the overall intention for the text? What leads you to this conclusion?

- Might there be one or more secondary intentions? Why do you think so?

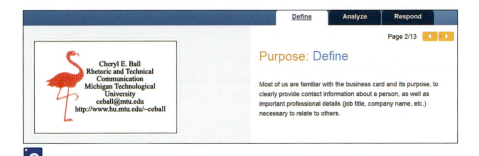

Figure 2.4 *ix: visualizing composition: Purpose*

Work through this interactive discussion for more practice with *purpose*. Visit **bedfordstmartins.com/writerdesigner** to complete this tutorial.

Context

Context can be quite broad, though it generally refers to additional information about a text, such as *where* the text is located (in an academic journal at a library, for example, or in the advertising section of a free weekly), *how* it is meant to be read (while sitting at a desk with one's full attention on the pages, or at a quick glance while flipping through a newspaper), or *what* surrounds it (similar academic journal articles, other advertisements, an article about dining in Seattle).

When analyzing context, consider these questions:

- What is the medium (print, CD, app, the Web, video, etc.)? Why do you think the author chose this particular medium over another one?

- Where did you find the text? What was the publication venue (book, newspaper, album, television, etc.)?

- What were the historical conventions for this type of text? What materials, media, or publishing venues were available at the time?

- What are the social and cultural connotations within the text? What colors, pictures, or phrases are used? What technologies does the text use?

- How will readers interact with this text? Will they read it on their phone or tablet while walking down the street? on a desktop computer in a public library? on a laptop in their backyard?

Figure 2.5 *ix: visualizing composition: Context*

Work through this interactive discussion for more practice with *context*. Visit **bedfordstmartins .com/writerdesigner** to complete this tutorial.

Author

Sometimes authorship will be quite clear—say, in the case of a signed letter to the editor—whereas at other times you will have to make an informed guess and rely on the implied author. Consider, for example, a newspaper advertisement for Starbucks. A team of graphic designers (the actual author) composed it, yet the audience assumes Starbucks (the implied author) is the one sending the message. There are other texts, such as a flyer for a concert, for which you likely will have no idea who the actual author is, but you can probably say a lot about the implied author based on the design of the text.

When analyzing authorship, consider these questions:

- How does the author (implied or actual) establish personal credibility? Do you trust this source? Does it matter?

- How does the author (implied or actual) come across?

- Does the author (implied or actual) have a certain reputation? Does the text work to support this reputation, or does it work to alter this reputation?

- If you know who the actual author is, can you find any historical or biographical information that will help you understand his or her credibility, character, and reputation?

Figure 2.6 *Wikipedia* **Home Page**

Wikipedia is renowned for its multiply authored and edited encyclopedic entries.

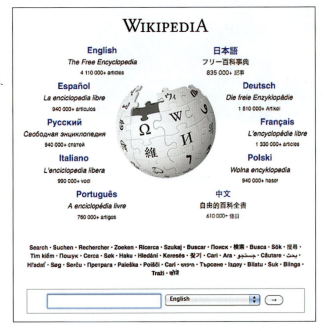

Genre

You've probably heard the term *genre* used to talk about static categories of texts in broad terms (sometimes related to the medium of a text), such as newspapers, albums, or movies, or in more specific terms—horror movies, romantic comedies, Westerns, and so on. Generally speaking, audiences expect something from newspapers that they do not expect from movies, and they expect something from horror movies that they do not expect from romantic comedies. This traditional understanding of genre helps us recognize how to group similar texts and understand their communicative purpose.

However, genres aren't just static categories; they can morph according to the local culture, the historical time period, the author of the text, the audience for the text, and many other influences. Think about the two maps we looked at in Chapter 1 and how different they are. Yet we're still able to recognize them both as maps, even though the genre conventions for an interactive online map and a print map may differ slightly. Genres are dynamic, but most genres have formal features that tend to remain the same in each use. These features are the **genre conventions**, or audience expectations, in the text. (We'll talk more about genre and genre conventions in Chapter 3.)

When analyzing genre, consider these questions:

- How might you define the genre of the text? Consider both a broad definition and a more specific definition.
- In what ways is the text similar to other texts within this genre?
- What key features make it part of the genre you've identified?

Is There a Right Answer?

You may never know everything there is to know about the author's intended purpose or audience. Additionally, there isn't always (or ever) a "right" answer when analyzing a text. What we can do is learn how to analyze texts so that we can better guess, hypothesize, or even create a theory about how a text works and why.

Rhetorical analyses can result in texts of their own (such as papers, presentations, or multimodal projects), but they can also function as research for your own projects. If you can analyze how a text works, you can often apply that understanding to the design of your own text.

Now that we've described the types of questions to consider when performing a rhetorical analysis, we're going to put these terms to action by analyzing the home page of the Washington State University Web site. This analysis can help illuminate how particular design choices are made in particular situations. Our goal is to figure out what types of **design choices** were used by the **author** to effectively convey the text's **purpose** to the **audience**. To achieve this goal, we also need to understand a bit about the **genre** and **context** for this particular text.

CASE STUDY

Analyzing the Rhetorical Situation

Figure 2.7 The Front Page of the Washington State University Web Site (October 2010)

Figure 2.7 shows the home page of the Washington State University (WSU) Web site. We're going to start our rhetorical analysis by thinking about this text's **purpose**, which in this case is closely tied to its **genre**. This text, like most university home pages, has two main purposes: (1) to serve as the portal to a large amount of additional information about the university and (2) to brand the university in a positive light. These dual purposes are what we would expect from a text within the genre of a university Web site home page. University Web sites tend to include attractive images and links to information about the university's academic and athletic programs, its admissions and financial aid policies, its students and faculty, and the town in which the school is located.

When it comes to the **author**, it is more useful to speak of the implied author (WSU) rather than the actual author (probably a person or group of people working in Web or information technology services on campus). Because the purpose of the page is to present a single informational view of WSU, no one person's name (or group of names) is listed on this page. The **audience** for the home page is the intended readership: people interested in WSU, including current or potential students and their parents, alumni, faculty and staff, or donors. A good designer would try to think of all the different reasons to visit the WSU home page and then design the page for these various users.

The Web site Design Shack did a study of fifty US university home pages from 2010 and concluded that the majority of them use the same ineffective design because they try to cram too much information into too little space. (In comparison, WSU's Web site topped the "Honor Roll" of best designs.)

We should also take into account the **context** in which this Web site was designed. Analyzing a genre within its *historical* and *technological context* is important—as our genre expectations change, so does the effectiveness of a particular design. This version of the WSU Web site was created in 2010 and is intended for viewing on a desktop or laptop computer. This genre convention—designing for larger screens—will likely change as the number of everyday users accessing the Web via handheld devices increases. For instance, consider how the very first Washington State University Web site looked in 1997 (see **Fig. 2.8**). Handheld devices barely existed at the time, and Web design principles were still in their infancy. The multiple, competing points of emphasis on the page (exacerbated by the overuse of crimson, a color that culturally draws our attention) and other design conventions of the period are no longer commonplace. Compare the 1997 site with the redesigned site from 2000 (see **Fig. 2.9**).

Figure 2.8 1997 Version of the WSU Web Site

Figure 2.9 2000 Version of the WSU Web Site

Contextually speaking, how do the 1997, 2000, and 2010 sites differ? Each of those sites looked good in its time, and many university Web sites have used similar designs in their histories.

In addition, the *cultural context* of a multimodal text can have a big impact on how we analyze that text. For example, the left sidebar in **Figure 2.9** includes a photo of a woman smiling directly at the audience. In countries that value groups over individuals, this photo would go against social customs and might be considered rude or even threatening. This is a good reminder that what we take for granted as a customary genre or genre convention in the United States (or in certain parts of it) may not hold across all cultures, social settings, or time periods. We can only analyze the WSU Web site's effectiveness in relation to its rhetorical situation, which has a unique combination of these contexts.

A university home page serves many purposes, and often appeals to some audiences more than others. Visit a university Web site's home page, and notice what information is emphasized on the front page. Why do you think this is the case? What does this say about who the primary intended audience is? What does the university assume this audience is looking for?

Do you see more information that sells the university (press releases, promotions for cultural events, a letter from the president) than you see standard university information (an academic calendar, application forms, a campus map, faculty emails)? How do you think this matters when it comes to the purpose and audience for this university's home page?

Process!

Analyzing Design Choices

Now that we know the rhetorical situation of the WSU Web site's home page—that is, its author, audience, purpose, genre, and context—we're going to examine how the author's **design choices** support the rhetorical situation. As we look more closely at the types of choices a designer makes, we focus on five key design concepts: **emphasis**, **contrast**, **organization**, **alignment**, and **proximity**. These terms aren't the only ones you could use to talk about choices—you may come up with some terms on your own or in collaboration with your colleagues—but to give you a start, we describe how these five design concepts are enacted through a variety of design choices. We call your attention to how these choices connect with the rhetorical situation described above, and we ask you to think about how such choices are or are not effective in this particular rhetorical situation.

Visit **bedfordstmartins.com/writerdesigner** to see an interactive version of our design choices analysis.

Emphasis

In speech or writing, emphasis means stressing a word or a group of words to give it more importance. In visual texts, it means the same thing; emphasis gives certain elements greater importance, significance, or stress than other elements in the text, which can guide your reading of the text as a whole.

Figure 2.10 **Primary Visual Emphasis on the WSU Web Site**

The three photos shown in **Figure 2.10** are given primary visual emphasis on the WSU home page from 2010. Simply put, they stand out. By emphasizing something bright, colorful, and positive (a smiling man, a picturesque wheat field, and a marching trombone from the WSU marching band), the author conveys the feeling of a happy and productive environment where people are filled with school spirit. Given that one of the purposes of the home page is to positively brand the university, this use of emphasis is an effective design choice.

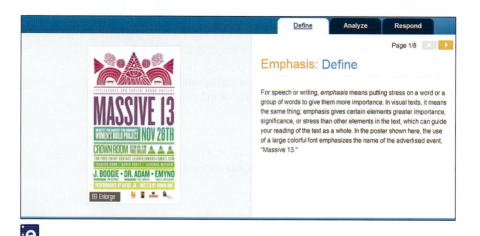

Figure 2.11 *ix: visualizing composition: Emphasis*

Work through this interactive discussion for more practice with *emphasis*. Visit **bedfordstmartins .com/writerdesigner** to complete this tutorial.

Contrast

Contrast is the difference between elements, where the combination of those elements makes one element stand out from another. Contrast can be determined by comparing elements in a text. Color, size, placement, shape, and content can all be used to create contrast in a text. Contrast plays a large role in emphasis, in that the most contrasted element often appears to be the most emphasized.

Notice how the WSU home page takes advantage of white space — a design technique that subtly employs contrast by leaving more of the background of the page (which usually lacks any elements other than a color or graphic) empty, making everything else on the page "pop." Thus, the page is not too busy, and the audience can easily find what they're looking for, be it donors looking for ways to give to WSU, a student searching for a professor's email address, or the parents of a potential student looking to learn more about the school's reputation.

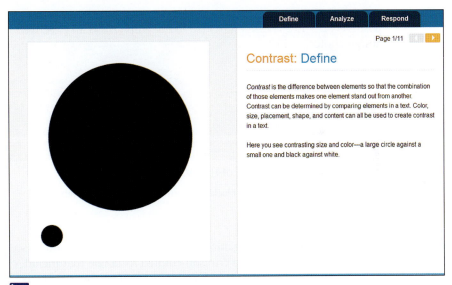

Figure 2.12 *ix: visualizing composition: Contrast*

Work through this interactive discussion for more practice with *contrast*. Visit **bedfordstmartins .com/writerdesigner** to complete this tutorial.

Organization

Organization is the way in which elements are arranged to form a coherent unit or functioning whole. You can talk about an organization of people, which puts people into a hierarchy depending on their job title and department, or about organizing your clothes, which might involve sorting by color and type of garment. You can also talk about organizing an essay, which involves arranging your ideas so as to make the strongest argument possible. Or you can talk about organizing the multimodal elements of a Web site to support the purpose of the text.

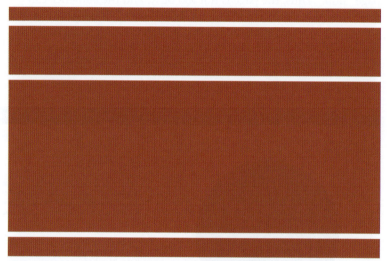

Figure 2.13 Organization of the WSU Web Site

This graphic represents the four blocks of information on the WSU Web site.

The WSU home page is organized into four rows of information (see **Fig. 2.13**). The first row is a crimson-colored rectangle that includes an index and a search bar. The second row includes the WSU logo, links to the Web sites for the various WSU campuses, and Quick Links. The third row, the one most emphasized, includes the three photos and the main topic links (About, Admission, Academics, Research, Services, and WSU Life). The final row includes a News link as well as links specific to particular audiences (future students, parents, alumni and friends, current students, faculty and staff). If we consider the purpose of this Web site as well as its audience, this organization appears to be effective in many ways.

Figure 2.14 *ix: visualizing composition: Organization*

Work through this interactive discussion for more practice with *organization*. Visit **bedfordstmartins.com/writerdesigner** to complete this tutorial.

Alignment

Alignment literally means how things line up. A composition that uses alignment to best effect controls how our eyes move across a text. Even if we're working with a text that is all words, every piece of it should be deliberately placed. A centered alignment—an easy and popular choice—causes our eyes to move around the space with less determination, as we move from the end of one line and search for the beginning of the next one. A justified alignment stretches the content so that it is evenly distributed across a row; thus the left and right margins remain consistent. This is a popular choice for newspapers because it can make a large amount of text appear neat and orderly. A strong left alignment gives us something to follow visually—even elements that contrast in size can demonstrate coherence through a single alignment. A strong right alignment creates a hard edge that connects disparate elements. Grouping things in a clear and interesting way can be useful.

Remember that we described the WSU home page as being organized into four rows. Notice how each row aligns with the other
rows. The crimson-colored row at top runs from the left to the right
margin, yet the linguistic content of this row is right aligned. The
remaining three rows are justified and run from the left margin of
the photo bar to the right margin of the photo bar. The only exception is the row of links center-aligned beneath the photos, yet these
links appear cohesive because they are encased in the photo row
itself (notice the white rectangle that encompasses both the pictures
and this row of links). The justified alignment makes the page feel
clean, crisp, and easy to use, which is important to an audience
looking for easy-to-find information.

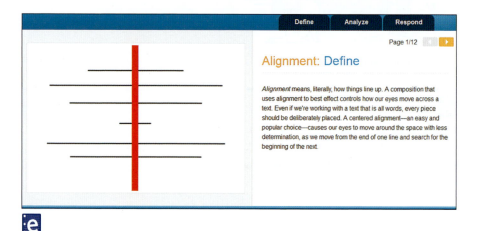

Figure 2.15 *ix: visualizing composition: Alignment*

Work through this interactive discussion for more practice with *alignment*. Visit **bedfordstmartins**
.com/writerdesigner to complete this tutorial.

Proximity

Proximity means closeness in space. In a visual text, it refers to how
close elements (or groupings of elements) are placed to each other
and what relationships are built as a result of that spacing. The
relationships created by the spacing between elements help readers
understand the text, in part because readers might already be familiar with similar designs of other texts. Proximity can apply to any
kind of element in a visual text, including words and images, or to
elements of an audio text, such as repeating rhythms or the verses
and chorus.

As described in the organization analysis, there are four major groups
of written links in the WSU home page. An audience member might

be looking for information specific to a campus or to an audience, so it makes sense that the author chose to place the items in each group close together; the words' close proximity to one another suggests a close relationship, whereas the groups themselves are placed farther apart. This design choice helps to make the page more usable.

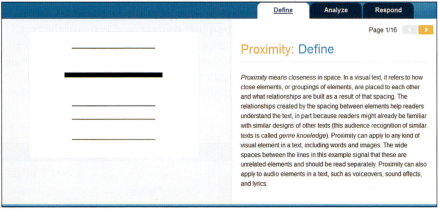

Figure 2.16 *ix: visualizing composition: Proximity*

Work through this interactive discussion for more practice with *proximity*. Visit **bedfordstmartins .com/writerdesigner** to complete this tutorial.

Process!

Visit your favorite Web site. Take note of the design choices that stand out to you, paying attention to the following:

- What elements does the design of the Web site emphasize? The logo? A certain picture? The navigation bar?
- Notice the organization of elements on the page. What comes first? What comes last? Why do you think the designer chose this order?
- How is contrast used on the page? Does the use of contrast help to emphasize certain elements? Does the use of contrast create a certain feeling? (Consider how certain colors can be used to encourage certain emotional responses.)
- What elements are aligned on the page? Does this alignment help you navigate the page? Does it cause your eye to travel in a certain direction on the page? Why might the designer have made this choice?
- How are elements positioned in relation to one another? Why do you think the designers of this page put certain elements in close proximity to one another while placing others farther apart?

Writing and Designing Rhetorically

We began this chapter by discussing the rhetorical situation and then moved on to the design choices. However, we can also work the other way around—starting with an analysis of the design choices so as to understand the rhetorical situation. Don't be surprised if analyzing a text's design (as we asked you to do in the Process! activity on page 37) causes you to go back and say more about the audience, purpose, context, and genre of the text. Examining design choices helps us learn more about the rhetorical situation. Doing a rhetorical analysis isn't always a linear or formal process, as the WSU case study shows—we could have written a lot more about the design choices or the rhetorical situation of the WSU home page.

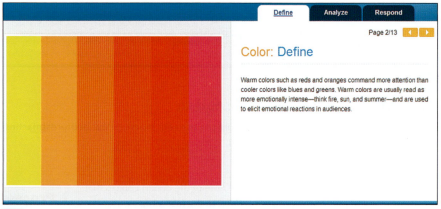

Figure 2.17 *ix: visualizing composition: More Design Terms*

There are also more design terms you can use to discuss a text's design. Visit **bedfordstmartins .com/writerdesigner** for more interactive tutorials on design choices.

Keep in mind that using rhetorical analysis to understand a text may result in a favorable opinion of the text but may also illuminate various problems—the rhetorical analysis may help explain why the text has that "wow" factor, or why it doesn't. For instance, consider if, instead of providing a few welcoming photos and easy-to-find links, the WSU home page were designed like an essay in a word-processing document. This primarily linguistic mode of design would be appropriate for an essay but would not be appropriate for the audience, purpose, context, or genre expectations of a Web site in 2014; thus, a Web page with this design would most likely be seen as a failure.

write/design assignment

Rhetorical Analysis of Multimodal Texts

Find three examples of multimodal texts that come from similar genres (e.g., university Web sites, talking cat videos, newspaper ads). If you already know what genre you're expected to produce for a class, project, or client, choose three texts from that genre. Perform a rhetorical analysis of the texts, whereby you describe each text's author, purpose, audience, genre, and context, and explain how different design choices are used to meet the demands of the rhetorical situation. When describing design choices, begin with the terms from this chapter: emphasis, contrast, organization, alignment, and proximity. However, you may realize other terms are necessary to fully describe the texts.

Choosing a Genre and Pitching Your Project

3

One of the best ways to begin thinking about a multimodal project is to see *what* has already been said about a topic you are interested in (or have been assigned) as well as *how* other authors have designed their texts on that topic. For instance, you may want to create a text about how students use technology to enhance their learning experience. Before getting started, you'll need to know what's already been said about that topic—an exploratory process that's similar to what you'd do when writing a research paper. Researching your topic is the *what* part of the equation (in other words, figuring out *what* you want to say). We'll talk more about doing research to figure out the *what* of your multimodal project in Chapter 4.

While you're researching your topic, you'll also need to explore *how* other authors are presenting that topic. What combinations of communicative modes do you see in other authors' texts about your topic? What design choices are they making? What genres are they using? Unless your teacher or client has assigned you a specific genre to work within, you'll want to research multiple genres in multiple media outlets—both academic (probably texts you'd find in your university library) and popular (texts you'd find on Web sites such as YouTube or in bookstores, trade magazines like *Good Housekeeping* or *Wired*, personal blogs, brochures in doctors' office waiting rooms, ads on the sides of buses, etc.). You'll see a different combination of modes and different design choices in each of these texts, depending on the rhetorical goals of the publisher and the author's rhetorical situation.

Figure 3.1 *Seasonal and Savory*, **A Food Blog by Angela Buchanan**

This genre of food writing features step-by-step pictures and instructions.

Figure 3.2 **A Recipe**

This genre of food writing can be found in different forms on food blogs and Web sites and in print cookbooks and newspapers, or can be passed down verbally through communities.

When examining the *how* of your topic, you'll need to ask yourself:

- How do other authors present your topic?
- Which of their texts seems to address its rhetorical situation most effectively?

In this chapter, we'll talk about how you can answer these questions by performing a rhetorical analysis on a sample set of texts about your topic, and then how you can use that information to decide which kind of text *you* want to compose given your own rhetorical situation.

Exploring the *What* and the *How*

Although we've referred to the *what* (the content of your text) and the *how* (the form your text takes) as separate things, it isn't actually possible to separate what you want to say from how you will say it. Your topic and your design are closely connected, which is why this book is called *Writer/Designer*. You can't be just a writer or just a designer; you're always both.

For instance, even if you're just posting an update to Twitter, you have to consider what you will say, how you will say it given who will see it, the context (the time of day, the event about which you're posting, etc.), and the ways that Twitter allows you to post supplementary information such as links or photos. Additionally, the design of Twitter's user interface restricts the choices you can make as you craft your tweet; for example, you can't post anything longer than 140 characters.

 Cheryl E. Ball @s2ceball   now
What you say cannot be divorced from how you say it. It's the same with all multimodal texts. #WriterDesigner
Expand

Let's look at an example to see more clearly how content and form are dependent on one another and on the rhetorical situation. Here are two texts that discuss the topic of video games and learning:

1. A scholarly book called *What Video Games Have to Teach Us about Learning and Literacy* by James Paul Gee, in which the author, drawing on lots of other scholarly research, argues that video games help promote literacy because they offer complicated, interactive narratives that game players have to learn to navigate

2. A prezi (an interactive, online, multimedia presentation application) called "Playing to Learn?" by Maria Andersen, in which she argues that using games in the classroom is an effective teaching tool because it engages students' brains in different ways and keeps them interested in learning tough topics (like math, which she teaches)

So, the *what* is that these two scholar-teachers agree that games are good pedagogical tools. And they give lots of scholarly and popular examples as to why games are good for us. In making our own project, we could cite either of these texts to support our own argument about games. Citing sources is something you probably have some experience with already (plus we'll talk more about it in the next chapter), so for now we want to focus on *how* these authors make their arguments.

On the one hand, Gee has written a scholarly book, although it's written in a style that's easier to read than most scholarly books. But he still relies on the genre conventions of scholarly books (like prose, citations, and formal language) to connect with his audience. There are visual modes used in his book—a few tables—but the text consists mostly of words formatted in a way that we're used to seeing in scholarly (or even popular) books. That is to say, his book looks pretty much like every other book in that genre (see **Fig. 3.3**).

Andersen, on the other hand, has chosen to present the same topic using a much different design: a media-rich, interactive prezi on the Web site Prezi.com. She also includes citations and examples, just like Gee does, although hers are usually much more brief because of the design conventions afforded by the Prezi interface. (We'll talk more in Chapter 5 about the impact of technological choices on designing multimodal projects.) However, unlike Gee, Andersen makes her argument about how games promote learning

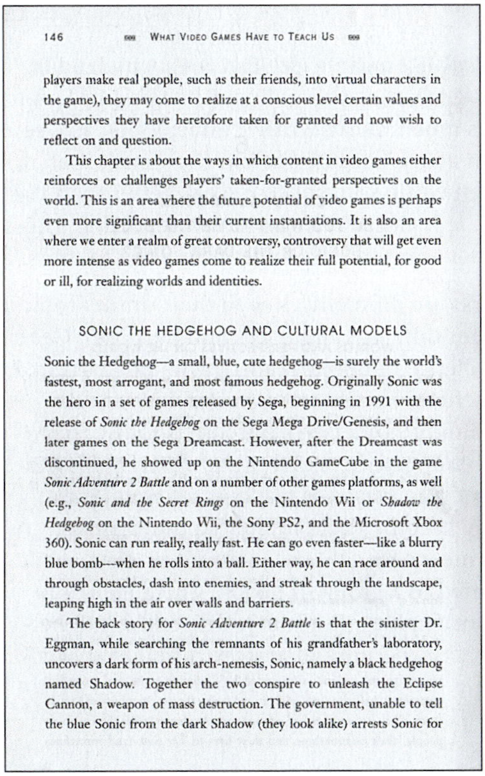

146 WHAT VIDEO GAMES HAVE TO TEACH US

players make real people, such as their friends, into virtual characters in the game), they may come to realize at a conscious level certain values and perspectives they have heretofore taken for granted and now wish to reflect on and question.

This chapter is about the ways in which content in video games either reinforces or challenges players' taken-for-granted perspectives on the world. This is an area where the future potential of video games is perhaps even more significant than their current instantiations. It is also an area where we enter a realm of great controversy, controversy that will get even more intense as video games come to realize their full potential, for good or ill, for realizing worlds and identities.

SONIC THE HEDGEHOG AND CULTURAL MODELS

Sonic the Hedgehog—a small, blue, cute hedgehog—is surely the world's fastest, most arrogant, and most famous hedgehog. Originally Sonic was the hero in a set of games released by Sega, beginning in 1991 with the release of *Sonic the Hedgehog* on the Sega Mega Drive/Genesis, and then later games on the Sega Dreamcast. However, after the Dreamcast was discontinued, he showed up on the Nintendo GameCube in the game *Sonic Adventure 2 Battle* and on a number of other games platforms, as well (e.g., *Sonic and the Secret Rings* on the Nintendo Wii or *Shadow the Hedgehog* on the Nintendo Wii, the Sony PS2, and the Microsoft Xbox 360). Sonic can run really, really fast. He can go even faster—like a blurry blue bomb—when he rolls into a ball. Either way, he can race around and through obstacles, dash into enemies, and streak through the landscape, leaping high in the air over walls and barriers.

The back story for *Sonic Adventure 2 Battle* is that the sinister Dr. Eggman, while searching the remnants of his grandfather's laboratory, uncovers a dark form of his arch-nemesis, Sonic, namely a black hedgehog named Shadow. Together the two conspire to unleash the Eclipse Cannon, a weapon of mass destruction. The government, unable to tell the blue Sonic from the dark Shadow (they look alike) arrests Sonic for

Figure 3.3 **A Page from James Paul Gee's *What Video Games Have to Teach Us about Learning and Literacy***

Looks like a book, eh?

Figure 3.4 "Playing to Learn?," Maria Andersen's Prezi about Using Games to Teach Effectively

Looks like a game, eh? Watch this prezi online at **bedfordstmartins.com /writerdesigner**.

by designing her text to *look like* a game (see **Fig. 3.4**), which adds visual, spatial, and gestural meaning to her linguistic text. Andersen doesn't have to present as much linear, written information as Gee does to get a similar point across because she has the visual, spatial, and gestural design of the text do some of that work better than the linguistic could do. Thus, *how* Gee and Andersen present their topics is as important as *what* they want readers to get from their texts.

Gee's and Andersen's works are different, despite their similar topics, because they are written for different audiences and purposes. Gee's purpose is to reach an audience of public readers who are interested in games and reading practices; he also wants to reach academics who study literacy and gaming. Andersen's purpose is to use the multimodal and interactive affordances of a prezi, which helps her create a gamelike experience, to persuade teachers that games can engage students' brains by keeping them interested in learning tough topics. One text is meant for solitary, in-depth reading, while the other could be presented to a group of people (since Prezi is a presentation tool) in a shorter amount of time. One text is not better than the other, in this case, because they serve different rhetorical situations.

Given the rhetorical situations for Gee's and Andersen's texts, why do you think they chose to use the modes that they did? Do you think Andersen could have effectively made her point through a scholarly written article? Do you think Gee would have been more successful if he had used an interactive visual mode instead of the book?

Process!

---

write/design assignment

Researching Your Project Idea

To narrow your topic idea and help you think about ways to design your multimodal project, use the following steps:

1. Find and read eight to ten texts on your topic, across a range of media.

2. List the arguments, points, or key ideas those texts offer about your topic. This is the *what*. For instance, in the examples above, both Gee and Andersen chose to focus on how teaching games improves students' learning. That's a key idea within the topic of games.

3. Next, list the genres, modes, and multimodal design choices (think back to the list of modes in Chapter 1—linguistic, visual, aural, spatial, and gestural—and the design choices in Chapter 2—emphasis, contrast, organization, alignment, and proximity) that the texts use. This is the *how*.

4. Analyze how the *what* relates to the *how* (using rhetorical analysis—context, author, purpose, audience, and genre), and decide which texts seem the most successful given their rhetorical situations.

5. Identify which themes in those successful texts most inspire you to do further research. (If a key idea seems to be missing from the list you compiled in step 2, that might also be a good place to do more research.) Shorten your list of themes down to one or two ideas.

Genre Conventions

You now have several new pieces of information to help you start building your own multimodal project: a few ideas for a suitable topic or theme; a list of texts that you can potentially cite, or that at least will inform the purpose of your project; and a list of multimodal texts that were successful in other rhetorical situations, which you could use as models when choosing your own project design.

One final thing we have to do before you start designing is to take a closer look at how authors know to choose particular kinds of texts or genres to work with in particular rhetorical situations. We talked a bit about genres and genre conventions in the last chapter, but here we're going to go into more depth about analyzing the genres of multimodal texts and figuring out how genre conventions work. If you learn to analyze the conventions of multimodal genres, you can apply that analytical skill to any kind of text you come across, and you will add more design choices to your rhetorical knowledge every time you compose a text for a new rhetorical situation.

In exploring your topic, you may have noticed that some of the texts used similar design choices in similar rhetorical situations. For example, if you analyzed breast cancer pamphlets, you probably found that almost all of them featured a pink ribbon and a script-like font. These are genre conventions that authors and readers use to make meaning within a rhetorical situation. It's important to analyze how these conventions are used within texts because genre conventions are a good starting place when designing a similar text for a similar rhetorical situation. They help us understand what audiences expect from particular kinds of texts in particular kinds of situations. For example, if you're making a breast cancer awareness brochure, do you need to use the pink ribbon in order to be taken seriously? Or are there good reasons to break with this genre convention?

Figure 3.5 Panel from *Understanding Rhetoric*, by Elizabeth Losh, Jonathan Alexander, Kevin Cannon, and Zander Cannon

This panel talks about comics while using the genre conventions of a comic.

Here's a different example: music. What are the conventions of songs that can be classified under the genres of rock, pop, jazz, classical, rap, disco, or country? Some classical music, with its soothing stringed instruments or mellow piano solos, might help relax or calm us, while disco's quick, pulsing beats and high-hat taps might energize us enough to dance. A site like Musicovery (http://musicovery.com/) color-codes musical genres and suggests certain genres depending on the listener's mood, which he or she can pick through an interactive mood tool (see **Fig. 3.6**). These tools—and our brains—rely on pattern recognition to classify musical genres. That pattern recognition is based on genre conventions. And while not every song within a particular genre uses the exact same conventions, being able to recognize the patterns can help us distinguish one song, and genre, from another.

Figure 3.6 Musicovery Web Site

This Web site helps listeners choose a musical genre and song based on how their mood matches a song's mood.

What If the Genre Is Unclear?

When researching texts for your multi-modal project, you may come across a text whose genre is unclear. If you don't know the genre of a text, remember that genres are created based on other genres, and on social circumstances and rhetorical situations that we're familiar with. That is, if you don't know the genre, ask yourself what the text *reminds* you of. Then maybe ask a few of your friends and your teacher the same question. It's likely that collectively you'll be able to identify a genre that most closely fits the kind you want to study further. Also, texts sometimes mash up multiple genres. For example, when social networking sites (like Twitter) were first created, they asked users to "microblog" in 140 characters or less, whereas blog posts are typically much longer than that. The term *microblog* shows that when status updates were new, they were compared most closely in genre to blogs. So if you encounter a text whose genre is new to you, see what other genres the text relates to and consider studying those as well.

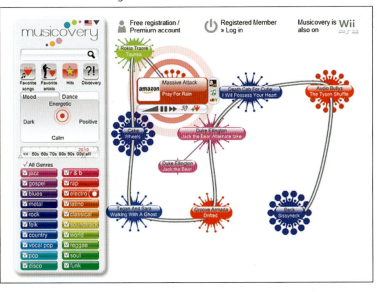

Process!

Pick a text, any text—it may be your favorite song, your office space, a restaurant, or your favorite movie. What mood does it put you in? What patterns does it have? How is it structured? Are the answers to these questions related? Consider other texts or artifacts in the same genre: Do they make you feel the same way? Do they have similar patterns or structures?

CASE STUDY

Looking at Genre Conventions

Here's how we might compare Andersen's gaming prezi with two other prezis about the same topic (see **Figs. 3.7 and 3.8**). We can use this exercise to figure out what genre conventions authors of prezis have come to use and have used successfully.

The Prezi software is based on our genre knowledge of other presentation tools (like Keynote and PowerPoint, which are in turn based on our knowledge of poster presentations). However, Prezi is also significantly different from other presentation software in that it allows readers to create zooming and animation features that are very difficult, if not impossible, to use in other presentation tools. For this reason, it is rare to run across a PowerPoint presentation that you're expected to interpret without any help from the author (e.g., notes posted online from a class lecture are still intended to go *with* the face-to-face lecture), whereas with Prezi you are more likely to run across presentations that stand on their own. Thus, that similarity across prezis becomes one possible genre convention, as noted in the table on page 50 (under "Does the text stand alone?"). We could list many more conventions in the table, but we'll leave it at these, just to give you an idea of how you might come up with your own comparative list. For example, based on the number of readers who have "liked" each of the prezis in the table, we might be able to judge the prezis' relative success, although such an evaluation doesn't do justice to some of the successful qualities within the two prezis that have zero likes so far. The more stand-alone the prezi is, the more successful it seems to be.

Of course, if you are required to create a presentation for your multimodal project and you know that the rhetorical situation requires you to deliver it personally, perhaps your presentation will still be successful even if your prezi doesn't stand alone. You just have to figure out *which* conventions are needed to make the text interesting and useful for your audience. For instance, the three prezis analyzed here use the standard linear navigation path, which allows readers to click on the right arrow to navigate to the next node of information, as opposed to the readers skipping nodes or the authors placing information outside of the

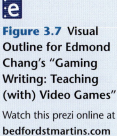

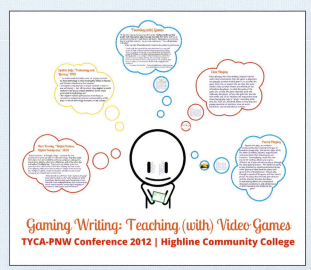

Figure 3.7 Visual Outline for Edmond Chang's "Gaming Writing: Teaching (with) Video Games"

Watch this prezi online at **bedfordstmartins.com /writerdesigner.**

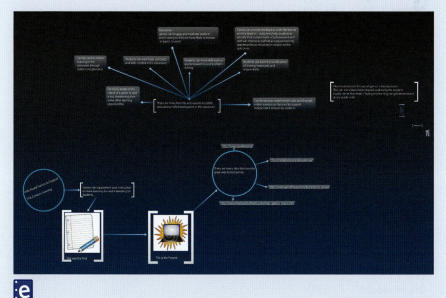

Figure 3.8 Visual Outline for William Maelia's "Using Web-Based Games to Support 21st Century Learning"

Watch this prezi online at **bedfordstmartins.com/writerdesigner.**

path for readers to discover on their own. The latter types of navigation would be more appropriate for readers to play with in a stand-alone piece than in a public presentation. The navigation path that your presentation uses is a design decision you have to make based on your rhetorical situation.

Prezi Genre Conventions

Prezis	Andersen's "Playing to Learn?"	Chang's "Gaming Writing: Teaching (with) Video Games"	Maelia's "Using Web-Based Games to Support 21st Century Learning"
URL (for reference)	http://prezi.com /rj_b-gw3u8xl/	http://prezi.com /ai6wnm0l_j1l/	http://prezi.com /yiknhf2wapi_/
Background color	White	White	Blue
Navigation	Left and right arrows	Left and right arrows	Left and right arrows
Use of words	Uses titles, quotes, and explanatory text	Uses titles, quotes, and explanatory text	Uses titles and explanatory text
Levels of zoom and rotation	Zooms in on key elements; rotation follows game board path	Zooms in on frame; no rotation	Mostly uses same level of zoom throughout (with a few variances); minimal rotation
Author	Bio and contact info in Prezi	Contact info in Prezi	No information in Prezi
Use of images	Images supplement the written text	Images convey an example	Very few images are used, and mostly for shock value
Path points	120	14	20
Does the text stand alone?	Yes	Yes	Yes
Use/purpose of navigational path	Path is designed around a background illustration that corresponds to the argument; great "bigger picture" view	Path revolves around central figure; "bigger picture" conveyed through thought bubbles	Path is based on mind-mapping concept, but not all nodes are related; some "bigger picture" purpose
Citations	Yes	Yes	No (but there is a resource list)
Number of reader likes	More than 1,900	0	0
Use of video/ animation	Yes (15)	0	0

Analyzing Genre and Genre Conventions

In the previous Write/Design assignment (p. 45), we asked you to come up with a topic idea for your multimodal project. You also came up with a list of multimodal texts related to that topic that you thought were successful. In this assignment, you'll build on that work to learn how to analyze genres and use that knowledge in your own project.

1. Go back to the list of successful multimodal texts you made in the previous assignment and pick one that you think best fulfills the author's purposes for that rhetorical situation. Do some research to find two or three more texts in that genre (they do not have to be on the same topic, although they might be). If several genres seem particularly appealing and successful, research them all.

2. Analyze the examples in this genre or genres and make a list of similarities and differences. These might relate to design choices such as layout, navigation, and multimodal elements, as well as to what each of those choices accomplishes within the text. You may also list rhetorical choices such as audience, purpose, context, historical period, etc. Refer back to Chapter 2 for a sampling of rhetorical and design choices that you might use. Also, see the Case Study on pages 48–50 for an example of how to create this list.

3. What design elements are similar? Do they look similar or function in a similar way across most of the examples? If so, you have a genre convention. Make a short list of all the conventions for that particular genre, which you should keep as a handy checklist when designing your own multimodal project in that same genre. (You'll also use it later in this book.)

Conceptualizing Your Project

Now that you have a better idea about the expected genre conventions and sources for your multimodal project, you are ready to put the *what* and the *how* together. You've already done a lot of preparatory work, so it's time to begin designing something on screen or paper so you can start to see how the pieces might fit together and get feedback from your instructor or client. Actually getting started can be a little intimidating, but we're going to give you two ways to begin conceptualizing your project: *representation* and *association*.

Representation

If you have writer/designer's block, try brainstorming some ways you could represent your topic idea using different modes. If you're creating a text about eating habits in different cultures, maybe your text could look like a plate with different kinds of food on it. Your goal is to find a way of representing your topic that adds meaning to your text. This is called a *guiding metaphor*. Maria Andersen created a guiding metaphor for her prezi that we saw earlier in this chapter: she used an illustration of a game board to represent her argument that games promote learning. The guiding metaphor adds meaning to her argument by actually showing, through visual, spatial, and gestural modes, how games can promote learning.

Representations don't have to be visual. For instance, if you're working on an audio text, ask yourself whether it's useful for your sound effects to exactly mirror the content of your narrative—should the cat meow like a typical cat in your piece? Or does the cat represent something else—a lion, a specter, a guardian angel—that might suggest a different sound effect?

Association

If you're having trouble coming up with something that *represents* your idea, try brainstorming things that are *associated* with your idea instead. This strategy can be helpful if the representations you're coming up with seem too literal or too specific (for example, if you're writing about love and the only representation you can come up with is a heart). Authors use associations all the time in everyday texts; how often have you seen Mickey Mouse's ears used to mean the Disney Company, for example, or heard the term "9/11" used to refer to the terrorist attacks in the United States on September 11, 2001?

For instance, Elyse (a student of Kristin's) wanted to work on a Web-based portfolio that showcased her photography and videography skills. While she had little trouble composing the photo pages, she wanted to find a unique way to link to her short films. With Kristin, she brainstormed the various genres, such as trailers, through which filmmakers showcase their films. But Elyse didn't have time to make a trailer for each of her short films (given the rhetorical situation of the assignment). She realized that movie posters would work better, since in a single glance a reader associates a movie poster as a stand-in to advertise a full-length movie. Elyse searched the Web for movie posters and began to compose posters for her films following the genre conventions (see **Fig. 3.9** for one example). Each poster linked to the film in her portfolio.

A big part of designing is to experiment with ways of combining content and form. This means that there isn't one perfect way to begin and it's perfectly OK (and normal) for your first ideas to need adjustment. Experimentation is natural. Coming up with several ideas as you conceptualize your project is a good strategy, because sometimes your first idea might be too literal or clichéd, or it just may not be what you want. Once you have a general idea of your

Figure 3.9 Movie Poster by Elyse Canfield

Kristin's student, Elyse, made this movie poster after brainstorming the best ways to visually link to her film projects on a portfolio Web site.

overall design, you can also use trial and error to flesh out some of the details. While the trial-and-error process can often take a long time initially, it makes for good practice in analyzing multiple modes in relationship to one another. Plus, the more you practice putting modes together and analyzing how they affect readers, the more quickly you'll be able to design your next multimodal project.

When you have a design in mind, record it quickly—maybe on paper, or with a video camera or voice recorder. It's not about how well you can draw or act but about getting the idea down in visual and spatial (not linguistic) form. Colored pencils or crayons are useful here if color is a significant part of the visual design. And although some authors are more adept at creating these visualizations on their computers, we find that most authors are more comfortable with using pen and paper because it's less of an initial commitment and provides a quicker way to brainstorm.

Process! Using pens, crayons, pencils, and paper—or a software program, if you prefer—brainstorm some ideas for your project's overall design; use one of the design suggestions listed above, if appropriate, or one of your own. Your designs don't need to be elaborate—in fact, they *shouldn't* be elaborate at this stage. They might just be flow charts or line drawings.

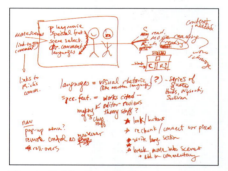

Figure 3.10 **Cheryl's Visual Design Brainstorming**

This crude drawing that Cheryl made visualizes the basic design of a collaborative webtext that she worked on and that was later published in an online journal.

Pitching Your Project

There is no single approach or kind of text that will work in all situations for all audiences. Knowing how to perform rhetorical analyses and looking closely for genre conventions will help you figure out how to write or design any kind of text in any future writing situation, but it's also key to look for guidance from others.

Figure 3.11 Matt Wendling's Pitch

Visit **bedfordstmartins .com/writerdesigner** to watch Matt's video pitch.

By explaining your project idea to your teacher, boss, or client before you really get started, you can be better assured that you're on the right track as you create a text for a particular rhetorical situation.

A **pitch** is a short presentation that explains how the *what* and the *how* of your idea might come together in the final project. It's a means of convincing audience members who have some stake in what you are proposing that you know what you're talking about and can take on the project at hand. (Pitches are sometimes called elevator speeches, drawing on the idea of a writer who is on an elevator with a publisher and has only four floors to convince the publisher to accept his or her book proposal.) Once an idea you've pitched is approved, you can start fleshing out the form and content of the project. In the next few chapters, then, we'll offer some practical suggestions for pulling all the rhetorical, generic, multimodal, and technological parts of your project together. In the meantime, the next assignment asks you to prepare a pitch for your stakeholders, clients, or teacher.

Keep in mind that at this point you have not completed a ton of research into the topic or designs, so there will be room for change. This is the same basic process used in writing essays; as you research and write more on an essay topic, the topic might become more concrete, or it might change direction, etc. In the case of a multimodal project, a change in topic or a refinement of your argument due to additional research might result in a rethinking of the project's genre and design—it's no longer as easy as cutting and pasting words into a different order. So you should expect some level of contingency in your project idea as your work progresses.

Stakeholders, Clients, Teachers, Audience—Who ARE All These People?!

Like the terms *writer, designer, author,* and *composer*—meaning the person or people who create texts, in this case YOU—the terms we use for the readers or recipients of those texts are multiple and may include *stakeholders, teachers, clients,* or *audiences.* We tend to use these terms interchangeably, but only because they are often dependent on the rhetorical situation for your text. Stakeholders, for instance, might refer to people from the community or from an organization on campus that you are working for or with, and each of these potential groups will have a different stake in your project. But stakeholders and clients may not be the primary audience for a project.

As one example, Cheryl has worked on projects funded by the National Endowment for the Humanities (an agency of the US government that supports humanities-based projects by providing federal grants to researchers), but the primary audience for those projects was other scholar-teachers. So, NEH is a stakeholder and expects certain kinds of reporting on such projects in exchange for funding, but the scholar-teacher communities in which we work are also stakeholders.

The term you use to refer to your multiple audiences will depend on the rhetorical situation. The important thing is to gather input from as many stakeholders as possible throughout the composition process. By pitching your project ideas early on, you can get a better sense of how to proceed. You should discuss the details of this rhetorical situation with your stakeholders before you embark on your pitch.

write/design assignment

The Pitch

Put together a pitch for your stakeholders. When planning your pitch, make sure you have these details about your project:

- What is the rhetorical situation for your multimodal project (as opposed to your pitch)?
- What genre will you use for your project?
- What is your topic? How will you convey your topic to your pitch audience? How much do they need to know at this point in the project, and what will you tell them to hook their interest? (How much more research do you need to do?)
- How will you design your project in relation to your topic? How is the design appropriate to your project's rhetorical situation?
- What do you need to know or learn so that you can complete your project? (In other words, how do you convince your teacher or client that you are able to complete this project in the time frame given for this multimodal assignment?)

You'll also need to think about designing the pitch itself:

- What is the rhetorical situation of your pitch?
- What genre of pitch does the rhetorical situation require (live presentation, stand-alone presentation, paper handouts, a formal written proposal)?
- What are the genre conventions you will use to pitch your project?
- Are there other requirements for your pitch, such as a time limit, a specific technology, or a dress code?

Working with Multimodal Sources

After pitching your project and getting the go-ahead from your teacher or clients, you'll want to start doing more in-depth research to flesh out your project's content, or the *what*, as we called it in Chapter 3. Working with multimodal sources and assets often requires strategies for collecting, citing, and sharing that are different from the research processes you may be familiar with. This chapter will discuss how to collect multimodal assets, what ethical issues to consider when collecting assets, and how best to cite multimodal texts. By the end of the chapter, you will have a list of the sources and assets you plan to use, an understanding of the ethics of this use, and citation information for your assets.

"On the Internet, nobody knows you're a dog."

Figure 4.1 Credible Sources Make You Credible

Finding and citing credible sources will prevent people from calling you a dog.

Finding Credible Sources

Every kind of text has a point to make and some type of argument it wants to get across, even if it's just to persuade the reader to pay attention to the information presented. For this reason, you need to think strategically about your sources. No matter what type of multimodal project you create — be it a promotional flyer, an informational Web site, a family scrapbook, or an annual report—you should ask yourself what kinds of sources, information, and evidence are going to be the most convincing to the audience you are trying to reach.

In all rhetorical situations, authors need to consider how best to build their credibility so that audiences trust their knowledge and character. This credibility is called *ethos*. Using credible and reliable sources is one of the most common ways of building ethos, and it is probably a tactic you've used when writing traditional research papers for which you were required to draw on "scholarly" sources such as books and journal articles. That kind of source material can be equally useful in multimodal projects, but you can also build ethos by having a well-designed project that pays attention to *how* the text works as well as *why* it works the way it does, as we discussed in Chapter 3. And the design comes not only from creating your own multimodal content but also from finding outside multimodal sources or assets (such as images, sound clips, Web templates, screenshots, photos, line drawings, and graphs) that can lend credibility to your project.

Below are some questions that you might use to evaluate whether your potential multimodal sources are credible. Some of the questions may be more important than others for your project. Remember that the credibility of sources will depend on your answers to the kinds of questions we have listed below (so make sure you can answer those questions in relation to each choice) and *also* on the rhetorical situation and genre of text you are producing.

- **How do you define credibility in relation to your project goals?** What makes a source credible can differ from project to project. For many projects, for example, a source is made more credible by having a known author. However, if you were composing a project about the human impacts of natural disaster, the inclusion of film or video footage shot by an unknown author in an affected area could prove to be highly persuasive to your target audience. The credibility of a particular source depends on your argument and the rhetorical situation for your text.

- **What is the purpose of your source? Does it seem biased in any way?** Is the purpose of the source to persuade? Does it seem evenhanded? Is it limited to one point of view? If so, should this affect your use of the source? Sometimes it works with your argument to use sources that are overtly biased, especially if part of your point is to illustrate how people with different perspectives think or act on a particular issue.

- **What information can you find about the text's creator and/or publisher?** Are the author's or organization's qualifications listed? If not, are they well known? Your audience's familiarity with or preconceptions about the author of a source can influence their response to your argument. For example, a video clip from CNN will probably seem more credible to your audience than one produced by an independent organization that they likely have never heard of. A report produced by a nonpartisan research group will generally be perceived as more neutral than one authored by a political party or think tank.

- **Have you seen this author or organization referred to in any of your other sources?** A source that is quoted or referenced frequently by other sources is generally one that other authors find believable (unless, of course, all those secondary citations are critiquing the original).

- **Is the information believable?** Why or why not? Consider also what type of person might not find the information believable. If the source seems suspect to you, or if you think it might seem suspect to a large number of other people, it likely will not seem credible to your audience. For example, if you need a source that explains the Second Amendment, a video that was made in someone's basement and has poor sound quality will probably be much less believable than a video made by a constitutional lawyer in her office.

- **What medium is the source in?** Researchers have found that visual evidence (like photos or videos) makes information more believable to audiences, but some audiences may question whether a visual is undoctored. Consider which media will be most credible for your project.

- **Are your sources diverse and inclusive?** Sometimes authors overlook diversity when considering sources, which can affect the credibility of their text with audiences. Considering diversity and difference reminds us to analyze our audience and to remember that we always have something new to learn from others. Make sure you aren't just interviewing your friends for an oral history project or choosing to represent only one gender or one race in a project that requires discussion of multiple cultures. Don't try to speak for a population that can speak for itself.

CASE STUDY

Multimodal Research Processes

Ariel was composing a genre analysis Web site for her digital media class with Kristin. (For more practice with genre analysis, refer back to Chapter 3.) The overall goal was to answer the following question: What strategies do different authors use to address a similar topic, and why do you think they use these strategies?

Ariel decided to explore Web comics that are based on the authors' real lives. She was already familiar with Hyperbole and a Half and Piled Higher and Deeper. Hyperbole and a Half is a simplistically drawn Web comic that humorously retells the life of its author, Allie Brosh. Jorge Cham started drawing Piled Higher and Deeper to chronicle his life as a PhD student.

Ariel was happy with these two choices but needed to find three more comics for her analysis. Her first step in looking for three more sources was to see whether Brosh's and Cham's comics had any links to other Web comics. Hyperbole and a Half did include links to Brosh's favorite humorous sites, but there was only one comic among them, and it was one that Ariel wasn't sure was based on real life. Cham included no links.

Ariel's next step was to do an Internet search for "Web comics." The third result in this search was a site called Top Web Comics, an archive of thousands of Web comics. Luckily for Ariel, one of the categories in this comic archive was "real life," though unluckily for her this category included 647 listings, and she only needed three comics. To narrow down her choices, she began to explore the comics while asking herself these questions about each one:

- What did she know about the text's author? Ariel needed to make sure that the comic somehow represented the author's real life; thus she needed to find some biographical information for the author in order to compare it against the comic's content.

- What was the purpose of the comic? The purpose needed to comment on the author's real life in some way.

- Who was the comic's intended audience? Ariel didn't necessarily need to know this before she could decide whether to use the comic, but thinking about it gave her a way to see how the different texts she was choosing might be part of the same genre.

In short, Ariel hoped to find comics similar to Hyperbole and a Half and Piled Higher and Deeper in that the author of each comic was closely aligned with the topic and the comic's purpose was to poke fun at everyday life.

After spending time looking at various comics and asking herself about the purpose, author, and audience for each (using the same rhetorical and genre analysis strategies we discussed in Chapters 2 and 3), she found three more comics that fit the bill: Johnny Wander, Questionable Content, and Girls with Slingshots.

Ariel now had five texts for her genre analysis webtext. For her research to be credible, she had to find comics that fit her genre subset and illustrate that she was knowledgeable about the comics' genre features.

Sources and Assets

You probably know the term *sources* already, but what are *assets*? Sources are texts, such as books, articles, Web sites, etc., that you can use to gather information about a topic or genre. Assets are the pieces of content that you'll actually use in your project. An asset might be a quotation, an image, a video clip, or a screenshot. For instance, let's say that for your project you need a twenty-second clip from a two-minute YouTube video. The source is the two-minute video (akin to a book or an article you pull from a shelf or the Web). The twenty-second clip that you pull from the video is your asset. You'll gather assets from your sources—and depending on your project, you may create your own assets (for example, by filming an interview with a friend).

Web sites and other digital media are updated frequently, so it's important that you save a copy of any asset you think you may want to use when you first find it. Things on the Web disappear. Jenny was giving a presentation about online adoption profiles and had planned to show a couple's Web site while she talked. She did not take a screenshot or save any of the images. Sure enough, the Web site was taken down the day before her presentation, and she had to scramble to find and analyze a new example. You can save screenshots of Web sites in an online bibliography program like Zotero or in your own filing system (see Chapter 5 for file storage and sharing tips).

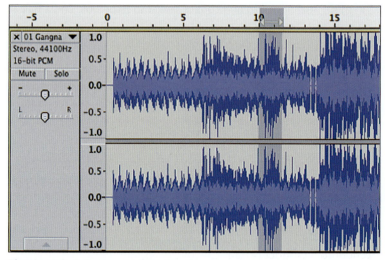

Figure 4.2 A Source and an Asset

In this waveform illustration of an audio clip, the entire song is the **source**, while the grayed-out selection between the ten-second mark and the eleven-and-a-half-second mark is the **asset** that will be used in the project.

write/design assignment

A Multimodal Annotated Source List, Part 1

Gather the texts you used in Chapter 3 to research your project idea. Use the questions in the credibility section on pages 58–60 to make sure that your sources are appropriate and that they will build your ethos as an author. If you need to find more credible sources, talk to your instructor, classmates, stakeholders, and librarian, and use the different text, image, video, audio, and other options your Web search engine provides.

Create a list in which you annotate each source, including the following elements where possible:

- the source's author, title, publication venue, and Web address (if relevant). Later in this chapter, you'll be asked to turn this information into a citation, but for now just document enough information so that you, your collaborators, or your instructor can go back and find the source.

- the asset(s) you're planning to use from this source
- a summary of the source, including the medium it's in; a description of how the content relates to your project pitch, including any important/major issues it discusses that you can use to support your project idea; and any important/major issues the source leaves out that your project will cover

Ethics of Collecting Sources and Assets

As you search for credible sources for your project, you should be aware of some ethical issues associated with collecting lots of assets that don't belong to you. The majority of the ethical issues we'll address in this section relate to copyright law; those issues include the fair-use principle, obtaining permissions, and the use of copyrighted material that authors have purposely given others more freedom to use under certain Creative Commons designations.

Copyright

Copyright is a legal device that gives the creator of a text—that is, a work that conveys ideas or information—the right to control how that text can be used. For a work to be copyrighted, the United States Copyright Office demands that it meet the following criteria:

1. **Originality.** The work must be an original creation—though it's not really as simple as that, because a work that is an adaptation or a transformation of a previous work can be copyrighted.

2. **Fixity.** The work must be capable of being stored in some way. An unrecorded speech cannot be copyrighted; once the speech is written down or videotaped, however, it can be copyrighted.

3. **Minimal creativity.** The work needs to be at least somewhat creative. This category is subjective, but for the most part anything that includes some original work will be eligible for copyright protection. Very short works such as names, phone numbers, and recipes can't be copyrighted, however, because the amount of creativity required to formulate any of those types of texts is considered to be too minimal. In other words,

under copyright law "creativity" is considered to take some effort. How *much* effort is often a matter for lawyers and judges to decide.

The point of copyright is to give an author control over how his or her text is used. Authors are the only ones who can legally distribute and/or sell their work—in short, they are the only ones who should be able to profit from it. The moment an author "fixes" an original idea into a text, he or she immediately has copyright over that text, unless the author signs the rights over to another person or to a group such as a publishing company.

When you're composing a multimodal project, copyright needs to be a prime consideration. As you'll learn in the next section, some of your assets may fall under the guidelines for fair use, but if you plan to ever share your project, you need to make sure that you observe general copyright principles. Sometimes it's easy to forget about copyright because of how easy it is to find images or songs through a quick Web search. But just because you find a source online doesn't mean that it is copyright-free. When planning your asset list, make sure you note who the copyright holders of your sources are.

Fair Use

Having to consider copyright law for your multimodal project may make you feel as though your creativity is being limited, but you need to remember that copyright exists in large part to protect an author's original work—and you may be very protective of your own work. However, while copyright does exist to protect original authors, the fair-use doctrine limits an author's total control.

The principle of fair use was established to allow authors to use portions of other authors' texts without permission for educational, nonprofit, reportorial, or critical purposes. Anyone working on a multimodal project should pay attention to the rules of the fair-use game. Unfortunately, those rules aren't always clear-cut. But keep the following four criteria in mind, and remember that your usage of the copyrighted work should meet these criteria as stringently as is possible in order to qualify as fair use:

1. **The purpose of use.** Is the work being used for nonprofit or educational purposes? Is it being used for criticism, commentary, news reporting, teaching, scholarship, or research? Fair use looks more favorably on texts that meet these criteria.

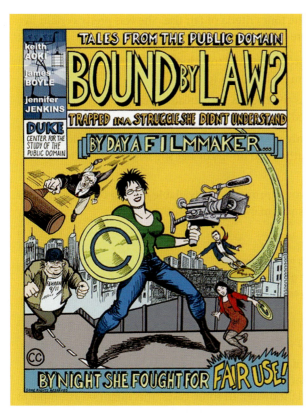

Figure 4.3 *Tales from the Public Domain*

Some works—usually those that are very old—aren't covered by copyright. These fall into what's known as the public domain. For more information on the public domain, read the comic *Bound by Law?* at **bedfordstmartins.com /writerdesigner**.

2. **The nature of the copyrighted work.** Is it factual? Has it been published? Fair use favors factual published works over unpublished works or forms of artistic expression.

3. **The amount of the work used.** The smaller the portion of the original text you use, the more likely this use is to be protected as fair use.

4. **The market effect of the use.** Will the new use of the text be available to a small group of people for a limited time? The broader the distribution, the less likely fair use will come into effect.

Think back to Ariel, who was working on a Web comic analysis. She created an "asset list" that included a screenshot of each Web comic's masthead as well as screenshots of different panels from the comics themselves. In thinking about these screenshots, Ariel had to keep in mind the four criteria of fair use. She was pretty certain her screenshots were OK, for several reasons:

1. The texts would be used for educational purposes—specifically, for criticism and analysis (purpose of use).

2. The comics themselves had already been published (nature of copyrighted work).

3. She was only using one image out of the entire catalog of comics each author had on his or her site (small proportion of the whole).

4. The text would primarily be available only to other people in her class (small market effect of use).

Process! | Search the Web for "fair use cases" and read about one or two cases that have gone to trial. Why was fair use upheld or not upheld in each case?

Permissions

In many cases, if you want to use part of a copyrighted text in your own multimodal project, you are supposed to request permission from the copyright owner. In some cases, this might be as simple as sending an email or a letter to a friendly author, who will reasonably grant you written permission to use the text for your project. For instance, although Ariel's plans for using screenshots of the various Web comics safely met the fair-use criteria for copyright, she also thought she would eventually use her webtext in her job portfolio, so she needed permission from the authors to use screenshots of their comics and an image of each comic's logo or masthead. The authors wrote back and granted her permission, and Ariel was able to move ahead with her project without fear of violating copyright law.

On the other hand, getting permission from some copyright holders can be overly complicated, expensive, and potentially unnecessary (depending on whether your use of the material is fair). For instance, Courteney, an author who was composing a video-based analysis of action films and who wanted to cite scenes from *The Dark Knight* and other Hollywood movies in her project, discovered that she would have to fill out a lengthy permission form supplied by the films' production company, Warner Brothers, and include a proposal explaining her use of each clip from each Warner Brothers movie. In addition, Courteney would not have been able to use or edit any clips from these movies without first getting approval

Figure 4.4 A Page from Ariel's Webtext Illustrating Her Use of Comic Screenshots

and (most likely) paying a fee. Most DIY multimodal projects (like the kind we discuss in this book) don't have a budget, so requesting permission and paying for the use of clips can raise more ethical and economic issues than it solves. That's when we encourage you to exercise your fair-use rights, transforming an asset for your project by critiquing or studying it for academic purposes, parodying it (among other appropriate fair uses), or using more permissions-friendly clips from a Creative Commons or similar search (discussed below).

Creative Commons

Confused about copyright, fair use, and permissions? Try Creative Commons, a nonprofit organization devoted to giving authors more control over how their work is used. Creative Commons (CC) also provides researchers with a massive collection of assets that are easily searchable and that can be used without worrying about strict copyright laws, ensuring fair use, or asking

When Humans Are the Text

You may need a different kind of permission if you are interviewing a person about his or her personal attitudes, beliefs, experiences, etc. Most organizations (institutions of higher learning, in particular) require you to have your project approved by the local institutional review board (IRB) if the project involves research that experiments on people or asks personal questions of people, *and* if you plan on **making the project public**. IRBs exist to make sure that certain research—in this case, human subjects research—is conducted ethically.

For a film that she was going to show only in class (a use that is *not* considered public), Courteney needed another kind of permission: that of the actress she wanted to film. She could have requested a signed consent form from the actress or obtained vocal permission recorded on film. If people are recognizable in your footage, you need their permission.

Visit **bedfordstmartins.com /writerdesigner** to download a sample consent form.

(and paying for) permissions. Authors can choose from six licenses, each of which is some combination of the following:

Attribution (BY): Users may copy, distribute, display, and perform the work and make derivative works based on it only if they give the author or licensor credit in the manner specified by the license.

No Derivative Works (ND): Users may copy, distribute, display, and perform only verbatim copies of the work, not derivative works based on it.

Noncommercial (NC): Users may copy, distribute, display, and perform the work and make derivative works based on it only for noncommercial purposes.

ShareAlike (SA): Users may distribute derivative works only under a license identical to the license that governs the original work.

So text licensed with an Attribution-Noncommercial (BY-NC) license can be used in your project as long as you give the original author credit. The other great thing about Creative Commons is that you can license your own work after you've completed your project. (If you use any CC assets with the ShareAlike designation, you *have* to apply a Creative Commons ShareAlike license to your project.)

Visit **bedfordstmartins.com/writerdesigner** to watch this video on the kinds of licenses Creative Commons offers users. What kind of license might work best for your multimodal project? Discuss with your stakeholders which kind of license your project might need. Make a note of which license would be best for your project and why.

Process!

Figure 4.5 Creative Commons Licenses

write/design assignment

A Multimodal Annotated Source List, Part 2

1. Add a "Rights" column to your list from Part 1.

2. For each asset you plan to use, designate one of the following choices in the Rights column:
   - **Get permission:** The asset is copyrighted, and thus its use requires permission. Include information for where and how to do that.
   - **Fair use:** Refer directly to the four fair-use criteria and indicate how your use of the asset qualifies as fair. Rhetorical analysis is a good method for indicating this use.
   - **CC-licensed:** Indicate which CC license this asset has and what uses the license allows.

3. If an asset needs permission, begin gathering that from the copyright holder(s).

4. For any assets you have that do not fall under fair use, try searching the Creative Commons licensed assets at http://search.creativecommons.org/ to find additional sources that might replace those copyrighted assets. Remember to look for assets that can be used commercially or can be modified, if these needs are relevant to your multimodal project. You might also consider creating your own original assets instead of using others, which we'll talk about more in the next two chapters.

Designing Your Citations

Strict citation rules such as those of the Modern Language Association (MLA) and the American Psychological Association (APA) often aren't useful when you're producing multimodal projects, because those guides were created for print-based scholarship such as essays, articles, and class papers. You *might* use MLA, APA, or some other citation style in your multimodal project, but that will depend entirely on your genre and rhetorical situation.

In this book, we have only two rules for citations:

1. Provide enough information about each source so that readers can find it themselves.

2. Use a citation style that is credible within the context of the genre you've chosen to produce.

Why these two rules? Because attributing your sources shows that you care about your readers, your text, and the authors whose work you're using, which helps readers interpret and even sympathize with your argument a little more—not to mention that it helps with your credibility.

Figure 4.6 How to Cite a Cereal Box in MLA Style

Visit **bedfordstmartins.com/writerdesigner** to watch Martine Courant Rife's video about citing a cereal box in MLA format. Citation styles can be quite malleable for anyone encountering multimedia genres.

Provide Enough Information for Readers

It's infuriating when someone you trust shares a link to an image (say, a lolcat) on Facebook or via email without including any additional context, and the link turns out to be "404 Not Found"—i.e., a dead end. The only thing you can do in that situation is to ask your friend for more information (if you cared enough to follow up), launch an image search of the entire Internet for the correct lolcat (if you don't know which lolcat Web site it appeared on), and then sort through the 427,000 hits to find an image that you *think* is the one your friend sent you. That's very frustrating. You (and your friends) should provide enough information so that readers will be able to find your sources or will at least know that you attributed your sources well enough to give credit where credit is due. And they'll like you for that.

Works Cited, Bibliography, References, Credits?!

Different style guides call your source list different things. You may have seen the source list called a bibliography. The MLA style guide calls it a works cited list. The APA style guide calls it a references list. A film or other media project would call the source list credits. What you call your list of citations (if you even have or need a list of all the citations in your project) will depend on what genre your project is.

Figure 4.7 Finding Missing Things

LOST DOG

Name
Male/Female
Breed
Coloring
Date last seen
Place last seen
If found, please call owner at
123-456-7890

Here are a few basic questions to help you start documenting your credibility with appropriate credits.

- Where is the source's home?
- What is its address?
- What is its name?
- Who is its owner?
- When was it born?

(Yes, it's sort of like finding the home of a lost puppy.) Let's try asking these questions about the screenshot in **Figure 4.8.**

Figure 4.8 Piled Higher and Deeper (PhD) by Jorge Cham

First of all, what is this asset's home and address? Let's say you ran across this image on Facebook and didn't know what it was, but you had a link you could click on so that you could read it in the context of the original site. You'd follow the link, which is the image's address (http://www.phdcomics.com/comics/archive.php?comicid =405), and from there you could discover the rest of the missing information. The asset's home is the Web site the comic lives on, and that Web site is called Piled Higher and Deeper. Note that the address of a Web asset is usually *not* the same thing as the main page, which in this case would be http://www.phdcomics.com/comics.php. For the purpose of citation, the main page is like the street name of a lost puppy's home—close, but not quite enough information to get the cute little thing back to its owners. So make sure you get the specific Web address and not just the main page address.

What is the image's name? In this case, it's the comic's title. In many Web sites, the title of a text that is part of a collection will be listed at the top of the browser along with the collection's name. If the title is not listed at the top, study the page to see if you can figure out what the title is. In this image the name appears both at the top of the page and in big letters on the comic itself: "Deciphering Academese."

Now, who owns this cute little thing? On a Web site that's designed like a blog or Tumblr, the author may not be readily evident, so search for links with words like *About* or *Author*, or look for a copyright note at the bottom of the page, which is where we find Jorge Cham's name. Cham is the owner of this comic. (Note that it's perfectly acceptable these days, depending on what genre of text you're working on and what its credibility standards are, to use assets that are owned by people whose names are weird little Internet handles like famouspoundcake or s2ceball. When you don't have the author's full name, use his or her handle.)

Finally, on blog-like Web sites such as this one, each post is usually tagged with the date of publication, otherwise known as its birth date. In this case, the publication date is January 18, 2004. Now we have enough information to track down the asset again, if we need to, and we can use the name, owner, birth date, home, and address to create a citation.

This screenshot is from a webtext (a scholarly multimedia article) published in the online journal *Kairos*. Track down the original webtext and create a citation appropriate for the genre of multimodal project you're working on.

Process!

Figure 4.9 Find and Cite This Webtext

Use a Credible Citation Style for Your Genre

This is usually the point in the production cycle where the MLA or APA style guide or *The Chicago Manual of Style* (CMS) gets pulled out—or more likely, a Web site that has examples of these citation styles gets pulled up. But for your multimodal project, you can't assume that you'll use MLA, APA, or CMS style. Instead, you need to consider what citation styles look like *in the genre* that meets your rhetorical needs. Here's an easy example: when you go to the movies, the soundtrack credits don't appear in MLA style at the end. Readers have come to expect that the sound citations in a movie will follow the format shown in **Figure 4.10**. Using this style makes the citations more credible because it looks professional, and it's easily recognizable by your audience. They know what you want them to understand when you use this citation style in a movie.

Not as common with a general audience but still functioning within its own genre conventions, the DJ Edit Pack also uses its own citation practices. An edit pack is a collection of songs, usually grouped by musical genre (punk, rap, electronic, etc.), that the DJ has altered in some fashion in order to make the track more dance floor friendly. These edit packs are generally used by other DJs who are looking for new music to play or include in their own mix tapes, though occasionally fans of the DJ will listen to the packs as well.

Figure 4.10 Music Credits in a Film

Figure 4.11 DJ Doc Adam's Edit Pack

Figure 4.11 shows a screenshot of Portland-based DJ Doc Adam's Punk Edits Vol. 1 Edit Pack. Notice the format for these citations. Each track includes the original artist, the song title, and the name of the DJ who edited the track (in this case, Doc Adam). While it's quite simple, it's the accepted convention for this genre. The point is: citation options vary as much as the genre and its features do. More likely than not, those citations look nothing like MLA-style citations. So this rule is about knowing your genre and figuring out how readers of that genre would expect citations to appear.

Process!

Visit **bedfordstmartins.com/writerdesigner** to watch the opening credits of the 1956 movie *Rock Rock Rock*. Then visit the Internet Archive (http://archive.org), where you can find over a million videos and other multimodal texts, most of which are available for download, remix, and reuse. Browse through some of the genres to see how credits have been designed historically. How are the credits for *Rock Rock Rock* effective for the movie's genre and rhetorical situation? How will the credits for your piece be different?

Figure 4.12 *Rock Rock Rock* **Opening Credits**

write/design assignment

A Multimodal Annotated Source List, Part 3

Return to your annotated source list and decide how your references should appear in your project, based on your genre. Consider what your instructor needs from you as well as the genre conventions for citation in your particular medium. If you need additional information to cite your sources properly, collect that information now.

Next, after choosing the format in which you want to provide your citations, compose a citation for each of your sources. Remember our two rules for citations: provide enough information about each source so that readers can find it themselves, and use a citation style that is credible within the context of the genre you've chosen to produce.

Make sure to add to your annotated list as you proceed with your project.

Assembling Your Technologies and Your Team

By this point you have an idea of the *what* and the *how* of your project, and you've found some sources that can help you get started. Now it's time to think about the practical steps you will take to start building your project. This chapter covers some possibilities for designing multimodal projects, asks you to consider the affordances of various technologies, and encourages you to think about the best practices for working in groups and sharing your assets as you proceed. In this chapter, we'll show you how to put together a technology review, a group contract, a project proposal, and a style guide. These documents will help you focus your efforts as you proceed with your multimodal project.

How Do I Make a Multimodal Text?

When it comes to building a multimodal project, there are hundreds of technology options to choose from. Any number of technologies may work best for your *current* project, but next month you might be working on a completely different project that needs a totally different piece of technology, so we can't just say "Use Dreamweaver!" or "Learn Movie Maker!" Instead, we're going to show you how to *learn how to learn* which technologies might be most useful for you in any given writing situation.

To figure out which technology is best suited to your multimodal project, you need to know what technologies are available. The short list of technologies on page 78 can be used to create or edit different media. The list includes some of the most common and most often used applications, but plenty of other software is available, and more is developed all the time. (This list may be outdated, as technologies change rapidly, but searching for some of these programs might help you find other, more up-to-date ones.)

Technology Choices for Multimodal Authoring

I need to design . . .	I can use . . .
Video	Windows Movie Maker, iMovie, Final Cut Express, Final Cut Pro, Avid, Adobe Premiere, Sony Vegas
Audio	Audacity, GarageBand, Logic Pro, Peak, Pro Tools
Images	GIMP, Adobe Photoshop, Adobe Illustrator, Picasa, Adobe Fireworks, Corel Painter, Adobe Lightroom, CorelDRAW, Microsoft Paint
Web Site	Adobe Dreamweaver, KompoZer, text editors
Blog	Blogger, WordPress, Weebly, Moveable Type, TypePad
Pages/Posters	Publisher, Adobe InDesign, most word-processing programs, construction paper, stencils, printer, scissors, ruler, etc.
Animation	Xtranormal, Blender, Adobe Flash, Comic Life
Slide Show	PowerPoint, Keynote, Prezi, Microsoft Photo Story, Google Docs Presentations
Screen Captures	Snapz Pro X, Camtasia, Snagit, Screencast-O-Matic, Jing
Micro- and Multimedia Blogs	Tumblr, Twitter, Storify, Pinterest, Jaiku

Remember that your multimodal project doesn't have to be digital. Many of the technology examples listed in the table above require screen-based presentations of your multimodal project, but that type of presentation may not be what you need. Perhaps you'll be delivering your multimodal project on posterboard at a meeting, or as a printed brochure, or as a flyer hung on the town bulletin board. However, even if you're planning to deliver your project on paper or in person, you may still need to gather digital assets and use digital technologies to produce it; for example, you may want to use InDesign to create a printed brochure.

When choosing a technology, you should also consider how people will actually view or use your final project. If you create a video, for example, you might choose to distribute it on a site like YouTube or on a DVD. We'll talk about distribution options in more detail in Chapter 8.

CASE STUDY

Assessing Technological Affordances

Ariel, whom you met in Chapter 4, was asked to compose a genre analysis Web site. She knew she wanted to compose a Web-based comic, but she wasn't sure which Web editor would be the best choice. Ariel had never done any Web design before, so she had to carefully think through what would work best for her given her project, her timeline, and her learning style.

Ariel knew she wanted to create a very simple Web site so that the comic itself would be the visual focus on the page. Someone reading a print-based comic can usually see many panels at once, but Ariel felt that her comic would be more effective if the user could see only one panel at a time. Because of this, she decided her Web page needed to have a slide show embedded in it. She also wanted to learn a bit more about coding in HTML, but she was hesitant to code from scratch since she had never done it before and had only a limited amount of time in which to get the project done. Given that she wanted a simple page and an embedded slide show and was willing to play around with code, she decided to search for a free HTML template that she could modify.

Ariel downloaded a template from freecsstemplates.org (see **Fig. 5.1**) and began playing with the code, using the basics that Kristin provided and tutorials she

Figure 5.1 Free CSS Template

Ariel used this free HTML template from http://www.freecsstemplates .org/preview/throughout. Ariel's final version of her site deleted the bottom section of the template.

found online. She edited the colors and headers to her liking and then inserted her comic into the slide show. Ariel knew a little about HTML and was willing to learn a bit more, but she wasn't confident about starting from scratch; thus the template was the best choice for her. While she was worried about the template looking a bit bland, the design of the comic itself gave her site visual interest.

Choosing an image editor for drawing her comics was significantly easier. Ariel knew she wanted a crude, hand-drawn look similar to that found in Hyperbole and a Half. Microsoft Paint, the program used by Allie Brosh to draw Hyperbole, would achieve the rhetorical effect Ariel was looking for and was easy for her to use, and she already had it on her home computer.

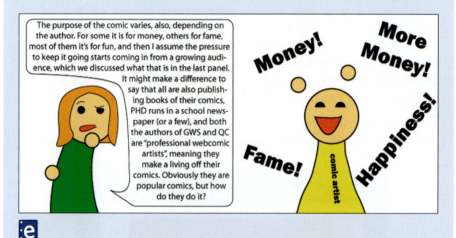

Figure 5.2 **A Panel from Ariel's Comic, Drawn in Microsoft Paint**

See Ariel's final Web site at **bedfordstmartins.com/writerdesigner**.

write/design assignment

Technology Review

Based on your project idea, review the table on page 78 and choose a set of programs that you think might be the best match for your project's needs. (Depending on your project, you may need several different kinds of programs, such as a photo editor, an audio editor, and a Web editor.) Create a chart for each technology or program you want to explore. In the left column of each chart, list the questions below.

- What does this tool do? What is its purpose? (Is it an HTML editor, a sound editor, a social media application, or something else?) What kinds of texts are usually made using this technology?

- Is the tool platform-specific (Mac/PC/Linux), or is it only available online?

- Do you have access to this software? Do you already own a copy, is it installed on computers in labs you have access to, or is it available as a free download or on a trial basis for a long-enough period of time for you to complete your project?

- How does the program work? (This is not meant to be a huge tutorial; just note the basic compositional or editorial features.)

- How steep is the learning curve, and will you have the time and resources to learn enough about the technology to complete your project? What are some tutorial sites or videos that seem effective for learning the basics?

- What do you need to do before you can start designing in the technology? (Do you collect assets elsewhere and import them into the program, or do you "record" directly into it?) Do you need additional technologies, like an external video camera or audio recorder, to make this tool function the way it's supposed to?

- What are the benefits of using this particular technology for the genre of your multimodal project? What are the drawbacks? What does the technology do or not do that will affect how you compose a text in your chosen genre? What file formats does it import and export?

As you research a particular technology, jot down your answer to each question in the right column of the corresponding chart. Compare your answers about the different technologies to help you choose the technology that will best suit your needs. If none are suitable, pick another subset of programs and begin your research process again. Then, based on the affordances you've listed in your chart, choose which program (or set) you will explore further to complete your multimodal project.

Going It Alone

You can create a strong multimodal project on your own, but there are a few useful things to remember. First, since you won't have team members to bounce ideas off of, be sure to do a thorough job in preparing your pitch presentation (see Chapter 3) and proposal (which you will do at the end of this chapter). Doing so will allow you to get critical feedback from your instructor, classmates, and stakeholders so that you can make adjustments as needed. All of these people can also review your mock-ups or storyboards (Chapter 6) and your rough cuts (Chapter 7) to help you realize your project's vision. Second, keep the size of your project manageable. Since you will be doing all the research, asset gathering, composing, and editing, you'll want to focus the scope of your ideas. Third, since you'll be solely responsible for the composing, seek out support for any technologies with which you're unfamiliar. We want to encourage you to try new genres, but if you run into trouble or have questions, consult with local resources, online tutorials, or friends. Just because you're working alone doesn't mean you can't get feedback or assistance from others.

Collaborating Effectively

Every reader of this book has likely had some kind of experience working with a group, and it's equally likely that not every collaborative experience has been a good one. As teachers, the three of us have certainly seen our fair share of group projects go awry, whether because of conflict over the topic or direction of a project, personal disagreements among members of a group, or group members who don't contribute what they're supposed to. We also know from the firsthand experience of writing this book together that collaborating is hard work, especially when you have people who can't meet together in the same place and who have strong opinions on the way things should be done. However, this book wouldn't have been the same if any one of us had written it alone. Collaborating with others, especially on multimodal projects, does have big benefits.

Guidelines for Successful Collaborations

Just as every multimodal project is different, so is every collaborative situation, but there are some common strategies you can follow to make your group experience more successful and productive.

- If you have the option, limit the size of your team to between three and five members. Larger teams tend to have trouble coordinating schedules and coming to decisions.

- If you get to choose your own team members, try to find others who will bring a diverse set of skills and perspectives to the process.

- Exchange contact information with the other team members, and commit to responding to them in a timely manner.

- Create a group or team contract to spell out member expectations such as roles, communication procedures, meeting guidelines, and problem-solving tactics.

- Be a good contributor—come to class or team meetings with all of your materials and with ideas about how to move the project forward. Just showing up and waiting around for someone to tell you what to do isn't really participation. And pull your own weight; nobody appreciates group members who don't complete their work.

- Be a good listener—collaborating requires that you listen to the ideas of others to hear what's beneficial. You don't always have to agree, but try to give people the chance to make their case.

- Remember that the most successful teams are often the ones whose members are flexible and are not so wedded to their ideas that they can't compromise. Being able to build off parts of one another's ideas can lead to some innovative and interesting possibilities.

- If your group faces *minor* conflict, try having a team meeting where members are asked to briefly share their perspectives on what's happening and their suggestions for resolving the issue.

- If your group faces *serious* conflict, talk to your instructor or supervisor, who will likely have strategies for helping to mediate and move forward.

Think about groups you have worked in that have been effective as well as groups that have not been so effective. Identify those aspects of group work that you believe help foster a positive work experience, as opposed to those that more often create problems. Write up a short list of dos and don'ts for group work.

Process!

CASE STUDY

Collaborative Composing Strategies

One of the biggest challenges of group work on multimodal projects is to find a way to meaningfully involve all group members and to divide work fairly and reasonably. The following case studies demonstrate how three student groups managed this challenge.

Dividing the Work by Project Sections

In one of Cheryl's classes, a student group created a webtext (a scholarly essay presented in multimedia form) about the visual rhetoric of movie posters in certain genres and across historical periods. The group collected visual assets such as movie posters, Web site assets such as free CSS templates, and scholarly sources on color theory and the history of movie posters.

The group decided that the project would have four main sections based on four movie genres and their representative posters: comedies, romantic comedies, action/thriller movies, and remakes. The four-person group divided the workload by movie genre so that each author was responsible for collecting assets and designing the Web page for a particular genre. The group members worked together to create the project's introduction and the works cited page. The group's working file structure shows the breakdown of the project's workload. (We'll talk more about file naming later in the chapter.)

Figure 5.3 Planned Home Page of the "Translating Movie Posters" Group Project

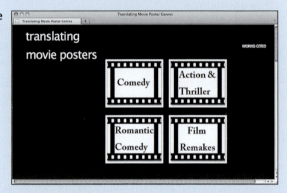

Figure 5.4 File Structure of the "Translating Movie Posters" Project

Organizing by Media Types and Expertise

Another of Cheryl's student groups also created a webtext, this one about fashion and identity. The webtext included original fashion photos, video interviews of the authors discussing how fashion *shows* their identity, and scholarly sources that supported the visual components of the webtext. The three group members chose to break down their drafting process according to each student's expertise. Darien, an art and design major, was responsible for the Web site construction; Jenna, a publishing major, was responsible for the written text; and Bridget, a technical writing major, was responsible for the video editing. Because each member played to his or her strength, this small group was able to compose a large, ambitious project in a relatively short amount of time.

Organizing by Compromise and Consensus

The final student group created an audio documentary on what it's like to be a search and rescue (SAR) team volunteer. The group was able to gather six hours of audio interviews, but then a critical issue emerged: How would the group decide which topics to develop and which topics to leave out due to time constraints? Each of the three members of the group approached the project from a different perspective: one of them wanted to establish an "intellectually artful" feel, one wanted "to make an emotional appeal," and one wanted "to create a coherent story."

To work toward meeting all of these different goals, each member listened to all six hours of audio and took notes on the themes and compelling stories he or she thought should be included. The group members were committed to compromise and worked together to decide on a few basic themes for the documentary. In the end, all of the members felt that they had been listened to and that their priorities had been accommodated. They all reported that the experience was frustrating at times but that their project was ultimately stronger because of the combination of ideas. Their final project was coherent and engaging, and provided a strong sense of the joys and stresses of being a search and rescue volunteer.

Figure 5.5 Don't Make Your Group Members Search For You!

Team Contract

If you are working in a group, you and your fellow group members should share and discuss your dos and don'ts lists from the earlier Process! activity. Use these lists as a basis for composing a team contract that spells out member expectations. At a minimum, the contract should address the concerns listed below. Depending on your group's rhetorical situation, you may decide to add other areas of concern to the contract. This contract will help hold your group accountable and will also help you write a project proposal (discussed later in this chapter).

Group Expectations

- What are our group goals for this project? What do we want to accomplish?
- What quality of work do we expect from each group member, and what strategies will we employ to ensure that we fulfill these standards?
- How will we encourage ideas from all team members?

Tasks and Deadlines

- What tasks need to be completed by when, and by whom?

Group Procedures

- What will be the dates, times, and locations of meetings?
- What is the preferred method of communication (email, a project-management system, texting, phone calls, face-to-face meetings) for sharing information about meetings, updates, reminders, and problems?

Personal Accountability

- Define each team member's expected level of responsibility for attending meetings, responding to communication from other group members, and completing assigned tasks on time.
- Describe how the group will handle a team member who does not comply with the contract. What are the consequences?

Organizing and Sharing Assets

If you're working in a group, or even if you're working alone but across multiple computers in a lab, at work, or at home, you'll need to find a good way to share your multimodal assets. Using a USB flash drive or an external hard drive can work in some cases—except when you lose it, forget to bring it with you, drop it, or try to save files on it that are too big. Online storage sites are a great alternative. These sites allow you to register (sometimes for free) and save files remotely on their Internet servers so that you can access the files from any other computer, smartphone, or netbook connected to the Internet. These sites are usually password protected, so you can back up your private files online (although the sites do come with security risks, so don't upload all your banking information!), and you can share project-based folders with anyone you are collaborating with.

No matter what type of sharing system you use, it's good practice to name and organize your files and folders clearly. Doing so will help you find items and keep track of which assets you've already edited, and it will also help other users collaborate, edit, or revise your project later, whether or not you're there. In this section you'll find some tips for naming, organizing, and sharing your assets. These tips are specific to certain kinds of media files. For instance, avoiding spaces and punctuation in filenames is useful when producing multimodal projects in certain kinds of technological systems (Web sites, audio files, etc.) but not as important with other types of systems (presentation software like Prezi or blogging platforms like WordPress). Although following a standard set of guidelines will ensure that your final project will work across all software and media types, you do have some flexibility in managing your assets depending on the genre, technology, and media you're using or producing.

Categorize Your Files Appropriately

Creating folders will help you keep your assets organized and will help you find them again when you need them, just as keeping your clothes organized in a dresser or on shelves makes it easier to dress yourself in the morning. Most effective folder structures are arranged in a hierarchy, with the broadest categories at the top and with the categories getting progressively more detailed as they go down. Follow these suggestions for using a folder structure to keep your assets organized:

- **Keep all of your project files in one place.** Some software programs require you to keep the files in a specific location. Research the requirements of your chosen software program and follow its instructions.

- **Create a folder structure** that will be easy to maintain throughout the design and revision process.

- **Name your files and folders** according to what they *are* and what they *do*. If you're using multiple images, sound clips, and videos, you might create three folders called *images*, *sound*, and *video*. (See the discussion of naming conventions in the following section.)

- **Create a separate folder for editable files** that won't go in the final project (we call these *working files*).

Use Good Naming Conventions

Certain types of technologies, such as the Web, rely on exact characters to find files. For example, if you save an .html page as "PuPPies .html," you will find it in a Web browser only by typing the exact filename—i.e., *not* "Puppies.html" or "puPPies.html." If you can't remember whether you capitalized the first (or second or third) letter, then you won't be able to find your file. Here are some best practices for naming files:

- **Use all lowercase letters in filenames.** If you know that you use all lowercase letters without exception, then you'll know to (1) name the file "puppies.html" and (2) look for "puppies .html" in your Web browser.

- **Use hyphens (-) or underscores (_) instead of spaces.** Web browsers and some multimedia editing programs can't read spaces, and/or they will translate them to a "%20" symbol (which nobody can understand), so it's best to avoid spaces entirely (as in the filename "student-interviews10-11.mov").

Figure 5.6 Be Careful When Naming Something "Final"

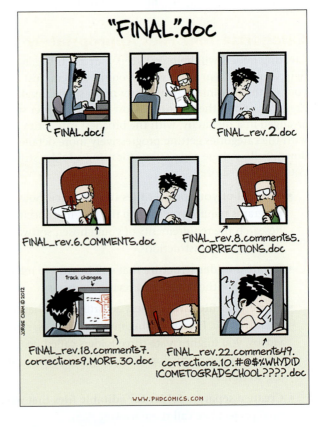

- **Be brief and informative.** Instead of naming an image "red_butterfly_on_fence_in_spring.jpg," consider using "red_butterfly.jpg" as the filename. Or simply call it "butterfly.jpg" if this is your only image of a butterfly.

Use Version Control

You will likely compile multiple versions of your assets throughout your project. For instance, you'll need to crop that audio track from two minutes to ten seconds. If you are exchanging files or using an online, shared repository such as Dropbox, using version control is especially important, so that you don't accidentally save over a revised version, causing you to lose new work.

- **If you plan to include dates in your filenames, decide as a group what date format you will use.** Will it be MM_DD _YYYY (for example, "clip1_10_23_2011.mov") or MM_DD_YY? Dates in filenames are OK, but everyone on your team needs to use them in a consistent manner.

- **Use an online version control system**—Git, Subversion, Mercurial, etc. (some of them are free)—that automatically assigns versions to your project files. Using these can be a little more complicated than just naming a file, but they will ensure that there is no confusion among versions, particularly if you are collaborating on different stages of a project. They also provide cloud-based backups of your work.

write/design assignment

Creating a Style Guide

A style guide is a set of agreed-upon standards that a group uses to write, design, and edit documents. Search the Web for "information architecture guides," "file-naming conventions," and "version control" to get a sense of what information you might include in your style guide. Discuss with your project team the best way to organize and share your assets, based on the best practices you have found through your research. Your style guide should include plans for naming, storing, and sharing assets as well as a brief description of why your group has chosen to follow this particular style, based on the technologies you plan to use and the kinds of assets you found in this chapter's other assignments. (Refer back to your technology review from earlier in this chapter and your source list from Chapter 4. You can use this style guide in writing your proposal, which we'll discuss next, and in creating documentation for your clients, which we'll discuss in Chapter 8.)

Proposing to Get It All Done

By this point, you have done a lot of work to brainstorm, pitch, and research the content and design of your project and to consider the best practices for collaborating. Now it's time to pull all that information together and map out in detail what you plan to do and how you plan to get there. It's time to write your proposal.

A **proposal** describes the scope of a project and how it will be completed. A proposal is a common and important document used to get suggestions and feedback on your detailed plan from an instructor, a boss, a stakeholder, or a client and to gain approval for moving forward with your project. Putting together your proposal will also be helpful as you move forward with designing and building your project; it's a chance to make sure that you have a solid plan, that you have all the materials you'll need, that you know how to use the tools you want to use (or have a good plan for learning how to use them), and that you have a realistic schedule for getting everything done.

Proposals can take many forms, such as business plans, cover letters for job applications, workshop and fellowship applications, conference proposals, grant applications, and even party invitations. Different genres of proposals have their own conventions, so when you're asked to put together a proposal for a particular situation, always research what kind of proposal will be appropriate and what sorts of information you'll need to include.

Whatever the genre of your proposal, however, here's some information that you should think about including:

- **Introduction/summary.** Give an overview of what your project is about, how you will approach it, what genre you will use, and how that genre fits the rhetorical situation.

- **Project plan.** Explain in detail how you plan on designing the project to support your argument; be sure to describe which technologies you will use, how you will gain access to or create media assets, and how you will integrate your research.

- **Justification.** Discuss why your proposed design is appropriate and effective for making your argument. (Your genre conventions checklist on page 51 in Chapter 3 will be helpful here.)

- **Roles and responsibilities, if you're working with a group.** Identify which group members are responsible for which project activities. If you have a group contract, consider attaching it to the proposal.

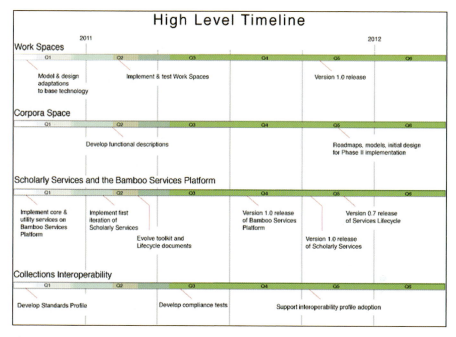

Figure 5.7 Example of a Timeline

This is an example of a detailed timeline from Project Bamboo, a consortium that builds technology infrastructure for humanities scholars.

- **Timeline.** Give a detailed work plan of how and when you will complete all of the project's components, including a breakdown of your tasks at each stage of the project:
  - doing further research
  - preparing a storyboard or mock-up (discussed in Chapter 6)
  - creating an asset list (discussed in Chapter 4)
  - preparing a rough cut or draft (discussed in Chapter 7)
  - revising and editing your final project (discussed in Chapter 7)
  - delivering your project (discussed in Chapter 8)

You'll notice that this list includes information about parts of the writing and designing process that you have yet to complete! If you haven't yet started drafting your project, how do you know how it's going to work? Well, you'll make an educated guess and leave yourself some space to adjust. Even the best-laid plans require adjustment once you get into the thick of developing them. Build time into your schedule to account for problems and readjustments, and be open to feedback on your plan.

Once you've completed your proposal and gotten feedback on it, you are ready to begin the drafting process by creating a storyboard or mock-up of your project. We'll help you to do that in the next chapter.

write/design assignment

Project Proposal

Write a proposal for your project that provides the basic information listed in the section above. Once your proposal is complete, get feedback from your instructor, classmates, stakeholders, and/or intended audience members. Use these responses to make refinements to your plan and to revise your ideas where necessary.

Designing Your Project

You've written a proposal and gotten feedback on your project idea from your instructor, classmates, and other stakeholders. You're ready to start drafting your multimodal project! But what will the drafting process actually look like? We're going to describe two different strategies for different kinds of projects: mock-ups and storyboards. These drafting strategies will help you create your road map to a great multimodal project.

A **mock-up** is a rough layout of a screen or page. It is most commonly used for drafting Web sites, but it can also be used for drafting any type of still composition that is primarily visual, such as a poster, an album cover, a brochure, or an instruction set.

A **storyboard** is a sequence of drawings, much like a comic book or visual outline, that represents the movement, spatial arrangement, and soundtracks of objects or characters in shots, screens, or scenes. Storyboards work best for projects that include a timeline, such as videos, audio pieces, or animations.

Mock-Ups

Essentially, a mock-up is an outline of a visual project. A good mock-up should include the proposed layout, colors, images, fonts, and recurring elements such as headers. Though mock-ups may include the actual textual content, often they do not. The idea is to create a kind of road map that shows where everything will eventually go, not to actually create the finished product. Web authors often compose mock-ups by hand, on paper, or in some type of screen-based software such as Photoshop. You can also create mock-ups using word processors, spreadsheets, or slideshow software. It's not so much how you create the mock-up that's important as it is *what* the mock-up illustrates.

Figure 6.1 shows a professional Web design mock-up for The Kitchen Sync, a boutique kitchen supply store located in Wenatchee, Washington. The clients (the owners of the store) wanted a Web site that would help advertise their store by providing a professional

Figure 6.1   **A Mock-Up Design for The Kitchen Sync**

This Web site mock-up shows how the basic features of the proposed site will look and offers different color options.

boutique feel while also showcasing the different products the store had to offer. The main goal was to get people to visit the store itself. While the clients had some ideas about what they wanted the site to look like, the Web designer wanted to show them a rough layout with a few different color and image options. Notice that on the left-hand side of this mock-up you see possible colors, textures, and images. On the right-hand side you see possible headings and buttons.

Mock-ups will also let you know where you might need to make adjustments *before* you put lots of time and effort into building your project. As writer/designers, we often find that our first ideas about how to arrange elements need tweaking, and they sometimes don't work at all. By first sketching out really rough layouts and then revising and making changes, we ultimately save ourselves time and create more successful designs.

The mock-up of a veterinary hospital Web site in **Figure 6.2** shows where the main content on each page of this site will be (where the picture and caption are now) as well as how the navigation will work within the drop-down menus at top and along the left-hand side.

Figure 6.2 Tapiola Veterinary Hospital Web Site Mock-Up

Mock-Up Guidelines

Here are some questions to consider as you design a mock-up:

- Is the proposed layout evident? Is it consistent across all possible iterations (pages) of the text? If the layout needs to change to indicate different sections or areas of a text, are those variations indicated in separate or supplementary mock-ups?

- Is the color scheme clearly indicated? Is it appropriate for the rhetorical situation and for readability?

- If images are used, is their relative placement on the page or screen mock-up purposeful and consistent across all versions?

- Are example fonts provided, and if so, do they adequately reflect the rhetorical needs of the text (e.g., did you use display type for headlines and body type for larger amounts of written content)?

- Are the navigational elements shown or indicated? Are they clear for users? Are they consistent across all iterations?

Taking into consideration the rhetorical situation for The Kitchen Sync mock-up in **Figure 6.1**, use the Mock-Up Guidelines to determine whether that mock-up is effective. Then compare it to the actual Kitchen Sync Web site at http://thekitchensync.com. Did the stakeholders make the same choices you would have made?

Storyboards

Unlike a mock-up, which represents a static text, a storyboard represents a text that moves through time, such as a video or an animation. Like mock-ups, storyboards may include rough visuals, but they use visuals to show the sequence of the text, as well as written descriptions of the actions or sound effects that need to take place at each moment. Storyboards can be incredibly complex but a simple storyboard consisting only of stick figures and a few arrows to show directionality can also be surprisingly effective. As with mock-ups, the important thing is not how artistic the storyboards are but that they indicate what elements (images, audio) and actions (movement, lighting, camera angle, etc.) need to occur at which point.

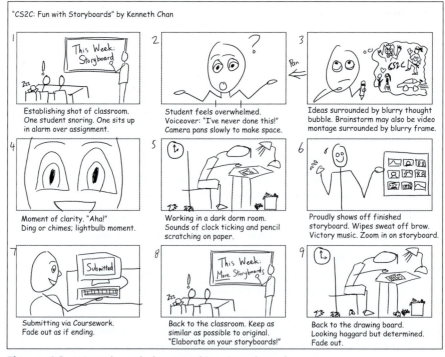

Figure 6.3 A Storyboard about Making Storyboards

The goal of an effective storyboard, no matter its level of complexity, is to capture as much information as possible and help you decide what shots you'll need to film, what audio you'll need to record, or what images you'll need to capture *before* the filming, recording, or animating begins. Similar to a mock-up, a storyboard can also help you get feedback on your basic design so that you can adjust it if it isn't working for your audience.

When creating your storyboard, you'll want to think about including notes on the following elements:

- Setting
- Movement by characters or objects
- Script/dialogue
- Soundtrack or sound effects
- Shooting angle

Of course, depending on the genre of your project, you may want to make notes on other elements as well.

For instance, Courteney was creating a three-minute video-based analysis on effective action films and had 64 panels in her storyboard. **Figure 6.4** is a small segment of Courteney's entire storyboard. You can see that you don't need to be an amazing artist to compose an effective storyboard; you just need to include enough detail so that your audience or instructor can figure out what you intend to do and give you feedback on it, and so that you have an outline to work with once you do start capturing your content.

Storyboard Guidelines

Here are some questions to consider as you design a storyboard:

- Is the initial setting or context clearly evident? How is each setting or segment change represented auditorially, visually, spatially, or linguistically—via intertitles, transitions, or other means?
- Is each character/interview/subject matter differentiated in some way (if it's necessary to do so)?
- Are important character or object movements indicated? (For example, if it's important that a character is seen rolling his or her eyes, have you used arrows around the eyeballs or something else to indicate that movement? Or if a car is supposed to exit the right side of the frame, how have you shown that?)

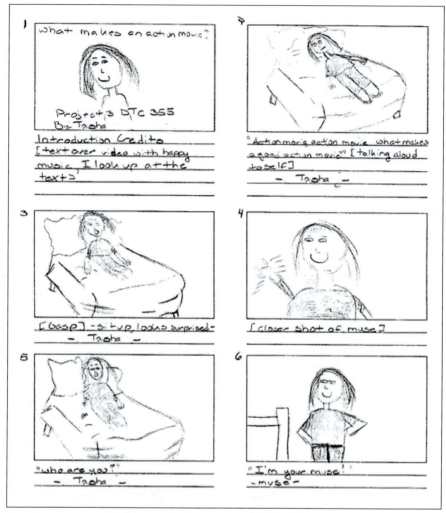

Figure 6.4 **The First Six Panels of Courteney's Storyboard**

These panels show her introduction of the topic (Panel 1), the beginning of her narrative-based analysis (Panels 2–3, in Courteney's bedroom), and the main characters in the analysis (Panels 4–6, Courteney and her "muse").

- Are snippets of major dialogue included underneath the story-board visuals? If not, what are the key ideas that need to be expressed in each scene or segment?
- Are sound effects or musical scores noted (usually under the dialogue or scene)? Do you indicate what these audio elements will be and how long or loud they will be?

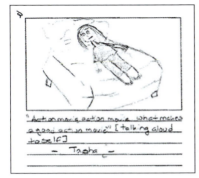

"Action movie action movie what makes a good action movie" [talking aloud to self]
— Tasha —

Figure 6.5 Courteney's Drawing of Herself in Bed (Panel 2 of 64)

Figure 6.6 Courteney's Video of That Scene

"I'm your muse." — muse —

Figure 6.7 Courteney's Drawn Introduction of Her "Muse" (Panel 6 of 64)

Figure 6.8 Courteney's Muse as She Appears in the Video

write/design assignment

Drafting Your Mock-Up or Storyboard

Are you creating a static, visually based project that would need a mock-up? Or are you creating a temporally based project such as a video, an audio project, or an animation that would be better served by a storyboard? Decide which method will work best for your text and begin drafting! Refer back to your genre conventions checklist and your conceptualizing documents/drawings from Chapter 3 to make sure you have included all major design features (or have purposefully *not* included them). Also keep in mind the guidelines for mock-ups and storyboards from earlier in this chapter, and make sure you've included everything you need for planning your project and for helping others understand what you are going to compose.

The Feedback Loop

After you've completed your mock-up or storyboard, you'll want to use it to get feedback on your project. Feedback can happen throughout the process and often results in multiple revisions. This process is rarely linear and is often referred to as a loop. That is, you share your project, receive feedback, make revisions and move forward, and then receive more feedback, continuing on until you and/or the stakeholders (ideally both!) are satisfied. You can also participate in others' feedback loops: your fellow students or colleagues may ask you to give feedback on their early work.

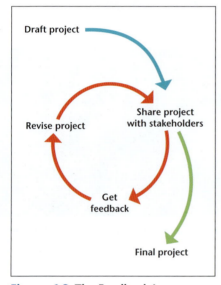

Finding out what your audience sees at this stage will forecast whether your design draft will successfully match what they want, need, and expect from the finished project. If your current plan isn't working, the feedback you receive should help you make changes to the draft and re-present it until the draft is on the right track for its rhetorical situation. You don't want to start composing the project itself if you're not sure it will suit the rhetorical situation. It's *much* easier to change a mock-up or storyboard than to change a finished multimodal project, so take advantage of your feedback loop.

Figure 6.9 The Feedback Loop

When you give feedback on someone else's design concept, you will want to consider a range of questions, such as those we listed in the Mock-Ups and Storyboards sections of this chapter, so as to ensure that the writer/designer's design choices are suitable for the rhetorical situation.

cover for an edgy literary magazine, so that the magazine would stand out among the other literary journals (**genre**) displayed on a bookfair table or store bookshelf (**context**). *Pank* also uses the cover image as a digital advertisement for the issue itself, which is another **context** the designer had to consider. For example, the editors of *Pank* change the magazine's Facebook icon to the issue cover for the run of that issue, and they promote the issue by posting the cover image in their Facebook followers' feeds. The cover needed to be simple so that it would stand out at a range of sizes and in a variety of media, yet it also needed to meet the needs of the intended **audience**: those who enjoy literary magazines and think of themselves as being on the cutting edge of literary arts.

The editor of the journal provided the designer with two possible photographs, both taken by artist Elena Duff, along with some information about the journal itself. The designer carefully considered this information and then designed four mock-ups (see **Figs. 6.10–6.13**).

Figure 6.10 *Pank* Mock-Up #1

Figure 6.11 *Pank* Mock-Up #2

Figure 6.12 *Pank* Mock-Up #3

Figure 6.13 *Pank* Mock-Up #4

After sharing the mock-ups with the editorial board (the stakeholders), the editor sent this email to the designer:

> Word back from all the editors is overwhelmingly positive, but with a strong preference for the second of the two girl/hair designs. While we like the playfulness of the other two designs, they feel a bit too disorganized/graffiti-like for our intended aesthetic. The hair designs feel a bit more serious while still keeping an edgy sensibility. The second of the two feels the most polished to us, and we like that it helps to emphasize the journal name itself. I'm wondering if I can see 2 or 3 variations on the theme, leaving the image(s) as is, but playing with the typography a bit? We'll choose a final design from this next round.

While most of the designs didn't make the cut, the designer was now able to focus on mock-up #2 (**Fig. 6.11**) and offered the editor a range of different typefaces for that design. The stakeholders eventually decided on the cover shown in **Figure 6.14**. As this example illustrates, designing a mock-up usually involves creating several options and playing around with design combinations to get a sense of what might work best for your text's rhetorical situation. Your first design choice is most often not the best or only way to get your multimodal point across.

Figure 6.14 Final *Pank* Cover

write/design assignment

Getting Feedback

Present your mock-up or storyboard to your instructor or other stakeholders for feedback. Your presentation may be formal (presenting to a client) or informal (conferencing with a teacher or workshopping with classmates), depending on your writing situation. Research the genre requirements for your presentation situation and prepare accordingly. (This may be similar to your pitch in Chapter 3.)

Be able to say why you've made the design choices you have—for example, you might explain that you chose the color scheme and navigation system for your Web site mock-up to match the interests of the site's intended audience, or that the nontraditional sequence of your storyboard's scenes is crucial to your text's purpose.

Refer to the checklists in the Mock-Ups and Storyboards sections to determine the areas that you might want your reviewers to focus on, and provide reviewers with your genre checklist (if appropriate) as they review your documents. If your stakeholders or colleagues offer feedback, assess that feedback for its usefulness in relation to your project's rhetorical situation, and revise your mock-up or storyboard accordingly.

Making Sure You Have What You Need

After you create your final storyboard or mock-up, you'll want to go back to your list of assets and sources and make sure it contains everything you'll need.

Assets

The following questions can help you plan for gathering and editing your assets, which you will do as part of the final Write/Design assignment for this chapter.

- Which assets do you need to spend time creating or editing in order to prepare them for your project? For example, you may need to capture video clips, crop sound files, or visually manipulate images.

- What hardware (cameras, sound recording equipment, markers, paper) and software (sound editing software, photo manipulation software, etc.) do you need access to in order to turn your mock-up or storyboard into a reality?

- How much time will it take to get these assets ready for your project? As with any project, especially ones utilizing digital technology, remember that you will almost certainly need some extra time to troubleshoot.

For instance, Courteney went back to her assets list and created the chart below to make sure she'd covered everything. In the "Needs" column she listed all the assets and other materials she needed for her project; in the "Solutions" column she figured out how to get them. Working from this chart, she made sure her room was clean, asked her actor friends for help in advance, and made sure the camera's battery was charged well before she set out to film anything.

Courteney's Assets Chart

Needs	Solutions
Bedroom setting	Use my bedroom when roommate is in class
Narrator (actress)	Me
Muse (actress)	Sarah, my friend in the theater department
Release form for actress	Get a sample copy from instructor; print out before filming with Sarah
Additional research on genre features of action movies, including: • which movies I want to use • how I will find/get them • credible sources to cite (either linguistic or multimodal) to support my analysis	• I own *The Dark Knight, Inception, Star Wars*, and *The Matrix* • I want to get copies (Netflix?) of *The Lord of the Rings* trilogy and *Terminator 2* • I will create an annotated bibliography of five print and multimodal sources (per my teacher's assignment requirements)
Video camera	Check this out from the school library (what are its hours?)
Video editing program for PC	I can't use the Mac lab at school because I work during open hours, so I'll use my laptop, which has Movie Maker on it

Timeline

Collecting assets sometimes takes longer than an author has planned for in his or her proposal timeline, whether because equipment or actors become unavailable or because deadlines for other projects and meetings interrupt the author's work. It's not unusual to have to repeatedly revisit a project timeline to make adjustments for different obstacles and constraints. Before collecting assets, authors should ask themselves these questions:

• Is this timeline still manageable? Think backwards from the project's due date and include any major milestones (internal, personally imposed deadlines or external, instructor- or client-based deadlines) that you need to meet.

- Are there any logistics you need to keep in mind as you proceed, such as computer lab hours or instructional technology check-out limits?

HOW WE MADE SNOW FALL

A Q&A with the New York Times team

The New York Times' astonishing Snow Fall: The Avalanche at Tunnel Creek, launched in the final days of 2012, capped a year of extraordinary work in interactive journalism, both at the Times and in newsrooms around the world. In the six days after Snow Fall's launch on December 20th, 2012, it had received more than 3.5 million page views and 2.9 million visitors, nearly a third of whom were new visitors to the Times website.

January 1, 2013

By Steve Duenes, Erin Kissane, Andrew Kueneman, Jacky Myint, Graham Roberts, Catherine Spangler

💬 25 Comments

Figure 6.15 Timelines for Complex Collaborations

Professionals collaborated for more than a year to make the *New York Times'* "Snow Fall" multimedia project happen. Read their process reflection at **bedfordstmartins.com/writerdesigner**.

write/design assignment

Gathering Your Assets

Revisit your source list from Chapter 4 and your proposal (with your timeline) from Chapter 5 to make a list of everything you'll need to compose your project: assets, tools, people to help you, etc. Use Courteney's two-columned approach, listing what you need in one column and where and how you'll get it in the other. Remember to follow the categorizing and file-naming guidelines from Chapter 5.

7 Drafting and Revising Your Project

Now that you have all of your assets gathered, it's time to make a rough cut of your multimodal project. A **rough cut** is one step beyond your mock-up or storyboard of your project: it's not your final draft, but you'll have your assets placed approximately where you need them in something resembling the program or technology you'll use to create your final project. Sometimes a rough cut is referred to as a prototype. Which term you use depends on what medium you're working in: *rough cut* tends to be used with timeline-based projects such as videos or audio texts, while *prototype* is more often used with code-based projects such as Web sites and software programs. In either case, this is a stage at which you can stop, step back from your project, and see whether it's all making enough sense for you to proceed as planned. That scene seemed like a good idea in your storyboard, but does it work on video? If not, your rough cut will let you know in time for you to figure out what, where, and how you need to revise so that the text *does* accomplish its purpose once everything is edited together cleanly.

Figure 7.1 Rough Cut of a Frog Sculpture

Figure 7.2 The Stages of Drafting, Frog-Style

Planning Your Rough Cut

Rough cuts are usually missing significant elements such as background soundtracks (with audio projects), transitions and intertitles (video projects), navigation (Web sites), permanent graphics (posters), and so on. In addition, rough cuts shouldn't include tightly edited assets, because feedback on your rough cut might indicate that you need to revise your project in a different direction. If you've cut your video down to a ten-second clip and then reviewers tell you they'd like to see a little more of it, you're out of luck. You want to have enough content left in your assets to be able to add different shots or material to your revised project if your reviewers suggest such changes. The following two lists include some examples of the *roughness* we mean when we talk about rough cuts.

Static Projects (Posters, Flyers, Brochures, Statues, etc.)

- The layout (spacing, alignment, number of columns, placement of headings, etc.) has been roughly determined. A draft of the written text or dummy copy has been placed on the document.

- Visual elements (photos, illustrations, logos, etc.) have been edited for size and placed on the document.

- Fonts, text sizes, and color schemes have been selected to provide a consistent look to the document.

- The project is available in a document/page layout program (e.g., Word, InDesign, Publisher, etc.) or in printed form (to test color) but not necessarily in the final output format (e.g., a PDF file).

Figure 7.3 A Sample Rough Cut

This rough cut of a video Cheryl is making has all the static photos and animated screen captures in their correct place in the video project timeline (see the upper left-hand corner). The sources are also included in the lower right-hand corner. Cheryl still has to add titles, a voice-over, and transitions between the visuals, but this version of the video is appropriate for a rough cut review, which viewers can watch in the preview window (in the upper right-hand corner).

Interactive/Animated Projects (Videos, Audio Projects, Web Sites, Presentations, Performances, etc.)

- All major pages, slides, screens or scripts, and/or blocking and settings have been found or created.
- Found or original multimedia assets have been edited for purpose and length:
  - graphics are cropped, compressed, and placed;
  - audio and video assets have been edited into smaller two- or three-minute (or two- or three-second) segments, cut down from those twenty-minute blah-blah-blahs of unnecessary footage you captured in order to get *just the right shot*;
  - ripped digital videos have been downloaded, and irrelevant portions have been edited out.
- Navigation/organization is in place but may not be linked yet (e.g., with a prezi, you may have the path in mind but have not

yet implemented it; with audio/video, you have rough edits in a timeline-based editing program).

- The draft is available for rough cut feedback in an editing program, off-line, or in an off-site workshop location.

Are you working on a type of project that isn't listed above? If so, what kind of project is it, and what elements of the project would be useful to include in a rough cut? In what program or technology will your rough cut be viewed?

Process!

---

write/design assignment

Rough Cut Feedback

Create a rough cut of your project. Have a colleague (not someone from your group) look at it to make sure nothing sticks out as odd, out of place, inaudible, nonsensical, etc. Remember, this is just a rough version of your project. The roughly edited assets should tell enough of the story or argument for your feedback loop to catch what (if anything) doesn't belong and what still may need to be added.

Moving from Rough Cut to Rough Draft

The difference between a rough cut and a **rough draft** is that in a rough draft all the assets should be finely edited and in place so that the project will work without any intervention by the author. That is, while your rough cut didn't have to work—it was a prototype of what you *hoped* would work—your rough draft should be usable in the technology and the medium that you will eventually distribute your project in.

How do you know whether your project works? Start by testing it yourself to see how easily an audience will be able to navigate and make sense of your text. You can gather useful information on how functional your project is and fix errors before the project goes to your audience. This is like proofreading an essay: the paper draft is done and you think it's ready to be turned in, but you know your teacher will catch

Usability Testing by Any Other Name

Throughout this book, we've referred to the feedback loop as a method for checking your work with your stakeholders. But you may be familiar with other names for this process, such as *workshopping* or *usability testing*. Workshops are usually considered a process that happens within a writing class and are a valuable part of the writing, design, and revision process. But since this book focuses on real-world projects, our feedback loop is more analogous to usability testing, which is a term you'd hear in technical writing and other professional circles. Usability testing asks real users—those people who are the target audience of your project—to perform certain tasks with your materials and report on their experiences. Since we suspect that users of this book are somewhere between the writing classroom and the professional world (if not in both!), we use *feedback loop* as a nice compromise. But really these terms all mean the same thing.

some places where you are missing transitions or have misspellings; so you print out the paper and read it through to try to catch those issues before turning it in. Preparing and testing the rough draft of your multimodal project has the same purpose. Here are some things to check for as you move your project from a rough cut to a rough draft.

❏ All written content has been finalized, edited, and proofread.

❏ All visual and aural elements (photos, illustrations, logos, videos, audio clips, etc.) have been edited in the appropriate software to their exact lengths or sizes and converted to the correct formats and resolutions, and they have been placed in their exact locations within the project.

❏ Fonts, text sizes, and color schemes have been implemented consistently throughout the document.

❏ Styles (when appropriate) have been used, and style guides have been followed.

❏ Animations (title screens, visual transitions, object movement, etc.) have been edited, synced for appropriate duration on-screen, and placed in their final locations in the project.

❏ Color photocopies of all visual elements have been printed at the quality needed.

❏ Soundtracks or other whole-project media elements have been edited for appropriate volume, added to the timeline, and synced to the individual scenes or navigation.

❏ Navigation or movement within the project (e.g., prezi path, slideshow autoplay, Web menu, performance blocking, etc.) has been created and finalized.

❏ Nothing is broken (e.g., images are in place, links work, videos don't stall, programs don't crash, etc.).

❏ The project has been exported from its editing program (e.g., Word, InDesign, Publisher, Movie Maker, iMovie, Audacity, Dreamweaver, KompoZer, etc.) into the final output format (e.g., converted to a PDF, MOV, or MP3 file; moved onto a Web server; etc.).

Preparing for Rough Draft Feedback

A useful review provides feedback on an author's in-progress (but hopefully nearly completed) work. When stakeholders provide feedback, they often intuitively understand the rhetorical situation and

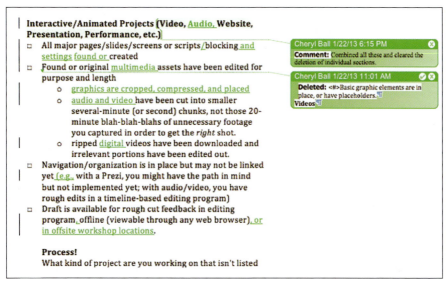

Figure 7.4 A Rough Draft in Microsoft Word

We had plenty of rough drafts for this book—more than twenty, in fact. Each time that we made revisions (using our editors as our feedback loop), we used the Track Changes feature in Word (as shown in this example). Once our editors approved the revisions, we cleared them out (by accepting them) and continued revising *other* sections that still needed work.

genre expectations of a text. Sometimes, however, reviewers don't know how to evaluate a project because they are not familiar with the particular situation or genre or because they are used to working on other kinds of projects. You can help a reader understand whether your project hits (or doesn't hit) the mark by providing them with a summary of the project's rhetorical situation; your summary should address some of the following questions:

- Who is the **intended audience** for this piece, and what rhetorical moves does the designer make to appeal to these readers/listeners/viewers/users? What suggestions do you have for further strengthening this approach or for better attending to the target audience?

- How well is the **purpose** of the project conveyed through its organization/navigation? Is there a coherent

How Will Readers Interact with Your Project?

As an author, you should be able to accommodate your readers interacting with whatever delivery method they might encounter your text through, as you prepare for them to give you feedback. Will they view your text on-screen? If so, what kind of screen will they view it on—computer, mobile handheld, tablet? Where will they view it? In the library, in their home office, in a classroom, on a train? Will they view it over a wireless or an Ethernet connection? Having them document this information for you will also help you troubleshoot any viewing issues.

message for the audience to follow? Do the authors offer some kind of commentary (the "so what" of the argument or story)? What suggestions do you have for adding or deleting content for the sake of clarity?

- How credible do you find the **sources** used for the project's argument? Were there any sources you found problematic? If so, which ones and why, and what would you suggest be used in their place? Were there sources missing that you'd suggest for the project?

- Are the **design choices** (emphasis, contrast, organization, alignment, and proximity) used in this project appropriate? If some seemed inappropriate in relation to the rhetorical situation, what suggestions would you make for revising?

- Do the **mode and media** choices contribute to the overall purpose and meaning conveyed by the project? Are there any you would add or delete, and if so, why?

- Does the project match expected **genre conventions**? If not, does it break those conventions in productive ways that serve the text's rhetorical situation?

Process! | Prepare a summary to provide to your reviewers, making sure that you address the questions above. Consider whether the summary should be delivered as a presentation, in writing, or in some other medium.

Providing Feedback as a Stakeholder

While you may be eager to hear commentary about your own project, providing feedback to your colleagues can be equally valuable in terms of helping you think about different and successful approaches to multimodal projects. As a reviewer of someone else's work, you have three main tasks:

1. to **read the text** from the perspective of a particular audience/rhetorical situation for which that text is intended (the summary of rhetorical situation and genre conventions is intended to assist readers with understanding this perspective),

2. to **evaluate** whether the text is successful at meeting the criteria/expectations required by that rhetorical situation, and

3. to **provide constructive feedback** to the author based on the text's (in)effectiveness.

Reading the Text

When reviewing a text, you should begin by familiarizing yourself with the rhetorical situation and genre expectations of the project. A summary or checklist like the one we recommended you create in the Process! activity on page 112 can be useful if you are unfamiliar with the genre, intended audience, or other elements of the rhetorical situation.

You may need time to figure out how the text works and why it works the way it does, and to discover whether there are elements of what the author has designed that you like (or don't like). Being an active reviewer—trying to figure out what the author's reasoning was for a particular design choice or rhetorical decision—will aid you in providing constructive feedback. In other words, don't just assume an author did it wrong. (Remember our lolcat from the opening chapter?)

Evaluating the Text

As you read, take notes on how and why you respond to the piece. This is where the summary of the rhetorical situation and genre conventions created by the author will serve as a touchstone for evaluating the project. As a reader, do you feel that the project meets your needs and expectations? Does it miss anywhere? For each question or comment that you pose to the author, you should be able to include discussion of "why" and "how" in your review.

Providing Constructive Feedback

In preparing your review from your reading notes, you should identify the main strengths and weaknesses of the project, summarizing your thoughts about how well the piece meets the rhetorical situation. Discuss how the piece meets (or doesn't meet) the project criteria, and provide formal and constructive feedback, including revision suggestions whenever possible. In many cases, rough draft reviews (rather than rough cut reviews) are written up and provided to the authors so that they can refer back to the review comments throughout the revision process. Here are some tips for writing a useful review:

- Use the beginning of the review to summarize the project's purpose back to the author, which helps the author see whether you understood the piece in the way that he or she intended or in a different way.

- Be generous in your reading, and be helpful and productive in explaining what's not working in the piece and how you think

Figure 7.5 Feedback on a Presentation

Cheryl watched this prezi by Shawn Apostel and recorded audio of herself giving him feedback. Visit **bedfordstmartins.com/writerdesigner** to watch the prezi, listen to the recording, and analyze Cheryl's feedback.

the author should revise the project. Use a tone that will help the author take in your advice rather than just be offended by it. Help the author recognize what is working so that he or she can build on those positive aspects in revising.

- The review should usually address revision suggestions in a hierarchical way, moving from the biggest issues to the smallest issues. Small issues are sometimes left out of the review if big-picture issues overwhelm the project. For example, it may not be important that a project has some grammatical errors if it's not hitting the mark as far as its overall purpose.

- Alternately, a review might be structured as a reader-response— that is, it might follow the reader's chronological progression through the text. But summaries at the beginning and end of the review are still helpful in contextualizing the reviewer's minute-by-minute commentary.

- Always explain why and how a project is or isn't working well, and make sure that your revision suggestions are clear, even if your revision ideas are more like suggestions than must-dos.

write/design assignment

Rough Draft Feedback

Ask your client, classmates, or instructor to review your multimodal project, and offer your services as a reviewer in turn. Before you begin, ask yourself (or your client) what the rhetorical situation of their project is.

- Where does the review take place?
- As the author, am I expected to be present during the review?
  - If so, what are the presentation expectations? Is it formal or informal? What is the expected attire?
  - If not, how will I provide reviewers with my draft?
- What technologies are available for them to review my project? For me to review their project?
- What's the timeline for reviewing? Will the review of each other's work take place at the same time? Do we each have a few days to review the work? What's the deadline?
- In what medium are the reviews to be conducted? If multimedia reviews are acceptable, is the author able to view reviews that are made in proprietary programs?

Using Feedback to Revise

Now that you have received feedback on your rough draft from your instructor, classmates, and/or stakeholders, it's time to evaluate the suggestions and make plans for revision. Try to consider *why* reviewers responded in the way that they did and whether there are changes you can make so that you get the kind of reaction you were intending. For instance, in the example we discussed in Chapter 6 (see pp. 100–102) the *Pank Magazine* cover designer had to revise some of his original design choices, based on stakeholder feedback, to achieve the rhetorical goals for his project. Remember, the reviewers had said this about the draft shown in **Figure 7.6**:

> The hair designs feel a bit more serious while still keeping an edgy sensibility. The second of the two feels the most polished to us, and we like that it helps to emphasize the journal name itself. I'm wondering if I can see 2 or 3 variations on the theme, leaving the image(s) as is, but playing with the typography a bit?

As the designer revised his mock-up to emphasize the name of the magazine, he aligned the image on the right and framed the logo *[Pank]* in the doll's hair. In his final cover, shown in **Figure 7.7**, *[Pank]* is also emphasized through the contrast between the heavy

Figure 7.6 *Pank Magazine* **Cover Draft**

The stakeholders wanted the designer to work from this draft of the *Pank* cover.

black font and the beige background. He also aligned the issue number in the curl of the bracket itself (draw an imaginary line from the top of the *n* in *no.* up to the logo and you'll see how the issue number is positioned). This helped to create proximity between the journal's name and the issue number, thus establishing a unified appearance so that the audience might more easily apprehend what they are looking at. The designer also worked to keep the cover edgy through the use of this photograph. The image creates an ethereal, eye-catching effect, and the fact that the doll seems to be reaching for the title of the magazine makes it even more appealing (and truthfully, a little creepy!).

Creating a Revision Plan

After reviewing all of the feedback you've gotten, you should assess which revisions are important given your project goals, noting that sometimes reviewers have bad days, or they don't understand your

Figure 7.7 Final *Pank* Cover, after Revisions Based on Editorial Feedback

rhetorical situation (because they aren't the intended audience). But don't let yourself be fooled into thinking that you are always right and that your project doesn't need any revisions. If a majority of your reviewers indicated that your font choice will give your audience the willies or that the tone of your script is condescending, they are probably right. In addition, if a majority of your reviewers didn't mention a particular problem, but one reviewer made a *really good argument* for revising and backed it up with evidence from your text and your rhetorical situation summary, it's likely that the suggestion is a good one, and you'll need to consider addressing it as well. Here are some questions to help you determine which revisions you need to make:

- What were the strengths of my draft that I should be sure to keep?
- What design choices were problematic, and how can I revise these?

- What rhetorical choices seemed out of place in my draft, and how can I better attend to my audience, purpose, context, and genre?
- What multimodal elements can I add or revise to strengthen the rhetorical effect and credibility of my project?
- What are the most important changes I need to consider as I revise?
- Given the time and technology constraints of this project, what can I reasonably revise before the next due date? What else would need revision that I don't have time to complete but *should* complete, given enough time and resources?

write/design assignment

Revising Your Project

Paying close attention to the feedback you've received and the revision plan you've created, revise your rough cut into your final project. Your task is to make recommended changes and put the finishing touches on your project so that it accomplishes all of your rhetorical goals. You will want to ensure that all of the multimodal elements you've included are purposeful and support the credibility of your project and that your audience can understand and navigate your text as you intend. Then test your project by using it in a venue as close to its final publication or presentation location as possible. Tweak and revise as necessary, until you're satisfied that the text does its rhetorical work and/or you're out of time.

Putting Your Project to Work

As you work toward revising and finalizing your project, this chapter will give you some additional considerations to make sure all of your hard work pays off. You want to be sure that your final product functions effectively for its context and audience. You'll need to think about how to distribute your project—whether in print, online, or on some kind of portable media format (DVD, USB drive, etc.)—and how to ensure that clients or future users of your project can understand your rhetorical and design decisions if they plan to continue developing your materials. Throughout this chapter, we offer tips for making your project **sustainable**, so that it will endure through changes in technology and (lack of) human interaction, particularly after you have delivered your project to its stakeholders and are no longer responsible for maintaining it.

Figure 8.1 Planning for Down the Road

It's good practice to plan for the future of your multimodal project well before the project is due.

Delivering Multimodal Content

When you reviewed your technology options in Chapter 5 (pp. 78–81), you considered the possibilities for distributing your final project. Read through the following list of questions and make some final decisions about who you want to see and use your project and how you want them to be able to access it. Some of these issues may require you to do additional research, but you can easily find information about things like file formats and access restrictions through a quick Web search. These kinds of questions, which cover access and storage issues, will help with the sustainability of your project—an issue that most multimodal authors have to address when working on their projects.

Who Will Use Your Project?

- Should access to your project be restricted to your client or audience, or should it be available to people who may not be part of your intended audience? When you upload a video to YouTube, for example, you can set it to be viewable by any user or restrict access to just the people you share the link with.

- Do you want to be able to easily share your project with friends, family, and potential employers (and are you allowed

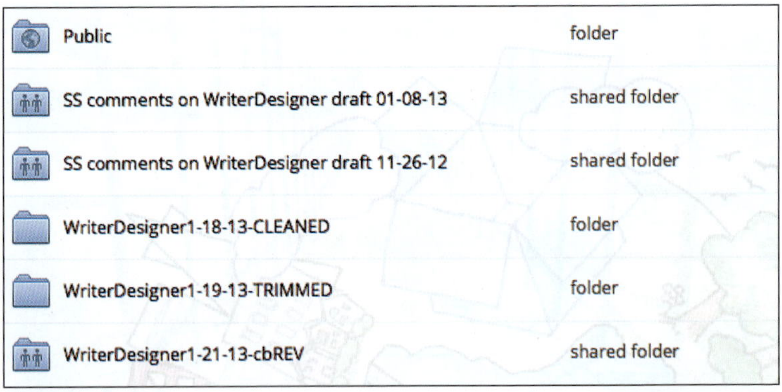

🔵 Public	folder
👥 SS comments on WriterDesigner draft 01-08-13	shared folder
👥 SS comments on WriterDesigner draft 11-26-12	shared folder
📁 WriterDesigner1-18-13-CLEANED	folder
📁 WriterDesigner1-19-13-TRIMMED	folder
👥 WriterDesigner1-21-13-cbREV	shared folder

Figure 8.2 **Sharing Files with Dropbox**

We used Dropbox to share a lot of the drafts of this book. The shared folders followed a standard naming convention we'd created. The shared folders were shared only among the three authors and our editor, whereas anyone on the Web could have accessed the "Public" folder.

to, based on permissions or confidentiality issues)? If you want to embed an audio or video project into a social networking site like Facebook, you'll need to think about file size and format.

How and Where Will They Use It?

- Will your audience look at a print copy of your project, an online version, or an electronic file stored in the cloud or on a CD, DVD, or USB drive? How will you get the project to them?

- Will your audience need any special software to view/use your project? For example, if you created a webtext in HTML/CSS, any Web browser will be able to display the files. If you developed an interactive animation in Flash, your audience will need to have the Flash Player plug-in installed in their Web browser. How will you make sure that your audience has this plug-in?

- Is your project platform-dependent? That is, will it run only on a Mac, or only on a PC, or only on Linux? Some programs export file types that are viewable only on a single platform. How will your audience gain access to the platform they need to view your project? Or can you create the project in multiple file types?

- What file format should you save your project in so that your audience can most easily access it? For example, if you've created an audio project, have you exported your final version as an MP3 so that it can be played on a wide variety of computers and devices?

- What resolution or compression quality should you use? If you are producing materials for print, their resolution should be a minimum of 300 PPI (pixels per inch). If you're creating a video that you want to be viewable on the Web, you'll need to carefully balance image quality with file size so that users can start to watch the video as quickly as possible but still see clear images.

Figure 8.3 A Project Gone Viral

Daughters of Ryan Cordell of Northeastern University started the Facebook page Twogirlsandapuppy in the hopes of convincing their father to get them a puppy. Cordell never expected the page to actually get one million likes, which it did in less than twenty-four hours. The family was invited onto *Good Morning America* within the week, got a puppy (from a shelter, another form of sustainability practice), and answered thousands of pieces of fan mail. Would you be prepared to follow through like this with your multimodal project?

Preparing for the Multimodal Afterlife

Now that you've finished your multimodal project, consider what will happen once you walk away from it. Unless you've set up a *Mission: Impossible*–style self-destruct option (warn your clients if you do!), your text will continue to have a life of its own long after you've forgotten about it. This can be both good and bad.

- **Good:** Maybe your "lolcats meowing 'Happy New Year'" video that you posted to a video-sharing site goes viral, and you and your cats get invited to appear on a late-night TV show. (Well, that could be a bad thing, too.)

- **Bad:** The photo album of you dancing at a New Year's Eve party, which you unthinkingly posted to your public Facebook account to share with your friends, shows up in a Web search by the human resources department for a company where you recently interviewed for a job that you really need. And they don't hire you.

- **Worse:** You already work for the company and they fire you because somebody in the background of one of those Facebook photos was doing something not just stupid or silly but illegal, and you're now a party to that illegality.

These examples relate primarily to **privacy** issues that all digital media authors need to consider, but authors must also consider **security** issues for the afterlife of their text. In this metadata-filled, face-recognition tagging, hacker- and spam-prone age, everyone should consider privacy and security. Even Cheryl, a supposed expert in digital media, had her server hacked—during finals week, no less, with all of her syllabi and course assignments on the server!—because she hadn't bothered to keep up with the security updates to the blogging software she had installed months or, in some cases, years ago. Getting hacked is just one example of a major security breach that can take days or weeks to fix, if it can even be fixed at all without deleting everything and starting over. And once you're done with a project (particularly if it's for a client or class, and only if you really *don't* need to work on it anymore), the last thing you want to worry about is starting over. So ask yourself the following questions.

Where Are Your Project Files Located?

- If they're stored online, is that online location private (password-protected and/or only available to a very limited group of collaborators or clients)?
  - Who do you want to continue having access to that private location? Remove/unshare/delete any users that should no longer have access.
  - Is the location secure enough to leave the files there as a backup?
  - What will you do if that backup location stops providing the service you're using? How often will you check back to see whether the service may be discontinued? Can you set up an automatic notification?

- Is that online location public (available on the Web for any search engine to scan or a potential boss to see)?

  • Do you need to have that final draft available publicly? If not, pull it down. If you do, perhaps you're not really done with this project, and you need to make plans (vis-à-vis financial or labor resources, time management, and other things outside the scope of this book's discussion) for maintaining it.

  • Does the metadata for the project allow a level of privacy that you're comfortable with now and will be comfortable with into the future? Will you be able to update the metadata to reflect your changing privacy needs as you get older?

How Long Are You Responsible for the Project?

- How often do you need to check into that location to make sure your privacy is being maintained?

- How often do you need to perform any upgrades or updates to the location to ensure your privacy and security? Can you set up an automatic update or arrange to be notified automatically when an update needs to be made?

- Should you copy online files (whether public or private) to an off-line location and delete the online versions?

  • Do you need to keep a copy of the files at all?

  • If so, what kind of storage device will you keep them on, and how will you ensure that you will be able to use that storage device five years from now? (Remember floppy disks? Zip disks? Probably not . . .) What is your plan for transferring your files to an upgraded storage device, or do you anticipate a time when you will stop caring about the files altogether?

Many of these questions depend on what the project is, how important it is that you and other people continue to have access to it, and what its longevity (its usefulness and rhetorical purposefulness) is expected to be. We're not all famous people who need our every digital file archived in the Library of Congress, but that doesn't mean we should just randomly delete stuff. Depending on your career path, you might need to create a portfolio of your work or refer back to an example or use an old photo in a new project. Be judicious about deleting—it should be a decision that is directly tied to the rhetorical situation of your text as well as to future, unknown rhetorical situations that are probable, given who you are and what you're likely to do with your life. Storage is cheap and getting cheaper all the time. Plus, you'll never know what you'll want to show your great-grandkids, nieces and nephews, parole officers, or cyborg pets in the future.

Take Responsibility for Your Stuff!

Yes, it might be annoying to perform regular upgrades to work we're no longer actively using, but that's the price we pay for having someone else keep copies of our stuff for us. Third-party hosting or sharing services are neither our mothers nor our guardians. They are not responsible for making sure our stuff is safe. Only banks do that (or at least we hope they do). And banks have insurance for those rare occasions when your stuff gets stolen. You don't actually get the items back; you get the monetary equivalent. But you don't get even that with free file-sharing or hosting sites or with social media sites; you only get lost projects and hacked accounts. So do the upgrades!

Figure 8.4 Keeping Content on Facebook

Should you rely on platforms like Facebook, Picasa, YouTube, and others to keep your valuable multimedia content safe? No. Always keep backups.

write/design assignment

Creating a Sustainability Plan

Use the questions on pages 120–124 to craft a sustainability plan for your project. This plan should include descriptions of where the project will reside (i.e., the storage and/or delivery medium), who will have access to it, what the access codes are (if any), and any other information relevant to the transfer of your project to your client. In other words, how will your project endure after you've completed it? For most of these questions, there is no clear-cut answer. Instead, it is a matter of weighing the pros and cons to find the solution that is best for your project's particular rhetorical situation.

Preserving Projects through Metadata

Deciding on a delivery medium for your multimodal project only fulfills part of the requirements for finalizing all of your hard work. Let's say your delivery medium is the Web, or more specifically a third-party hosting site such as Facebook, YouTube, Prezi, SoundCloud, or Wikimedia. You could just upload your project and walk away. As we discussed in the last section, you should tell your client where your project is located—but perhaps your client is not your intended audience! Maybe you've created a radio essay that you will turn in for a class project, but you also will upload it to a radio-essay Web site

Figure 8.5 StoryCorps Web Page with Metadata

The Web page for this Studs Terkel story contains metadata in the form of a title, a recording location, credits, a description, and other data.

such as StoryCorps. So your teacher is your client, but the Web site listeners are your audience. How will your intended audience actually *find* your project? How will other people know what it is? How will a computer, which can only scan text, search for your audio file? Metadata is the answer. **Metadata** is data about data: information about a piece of content that can tell a reader who created the content, what it represents, when it was recorded, and other bits of info that make your project findable and thus usable by others.

You've probably seen keywords, tags, categories, and other metadata on media-sharing sites like Wikimedia Commons. Each media element that an author uploads to Wikimedia Commons has to include written information or data *about* the media element so that Wikimedia can help other users find that element. Without this metadata, the media element won't be easily found by, say, a user searching for the perfect audio sound effect of rain falling in Glenshaw, Pennsylvania, to include in her documentary about that tiny town.

A screenshot of the summary section of the Wikimedia Commons page for the sound effect of "Heavy rain in Glenshaw, PA" (**Fig. 8.6**) shows some of the metadata for this one file. The metadata includes a description of the sound effect, the date it was recorded, the source of the work, the author who created it, what the file's permissions are, where the file was recorded, and a bunch of other information

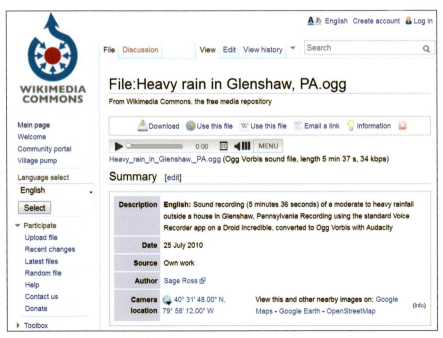

Figure 8.6 Finding Metadata on a Wikimedia Commons Page

further down the page. Researchers can search for the town name (if they need a specific geographic location), date (if they need a specific time period), and so on from either a search engine or from the Wikimedia Commons home page, where users can browse for content by topic, media type, author, copyright license, or publication source (among other options). All of this information is metadata that the file's author included when he or she uploaded the file to the Web. Additionally, supporting written material such as transcripts of audio/video files and descriptions from proposals can function as metadata for your final project. Including all of this information will help make sure that your project is sustainable.

Process! | What metadata does your delivery medium require? Which metadata do you need to create, and which can you access in your project's written documentation and reuse?

Documenting Your Design Process for Future Users

Documentation explains how a project was created or how to use it. There are many kinds of documentation, such as white papers, reference manuals, online help files, and user guides. Providing documentation is another way to make your project sustainable, as it helps your clients or stakeholders understand how you designed your project so that they can add to or revise your work in the future. This is particularly important for a project that you know the client *will* continue to revise after you've stopped working on it. Clients will often continue working on projects after you've finished designing them, especially if you're volunteering, getting paid with one-time grant funds, or participating in a service-learning class. Projects such as newsletters, training documentation, blogs, and other serialized or continually updated texts often have a series of people working on them, which increases the likelihood that the texts will remain active and useful for the stakeholders. Providing documentation is the best way to help the next person figure out how to carry on your work. There are many ways to document your processes. In the next few sections we explain two types of documentation methods: wikis and comments. Depending on your project, you may need one or both of those methods, or you may use some other method or combination of methods to convey your processes to your client. No matter which documentation method you choose, the rhetorical considerations we've used throughout this book will be effective when considering medium, genre, or technology.

Collaborating on Wiki Documentation

In **Figure 8.7**, you can see some of the documentation developed by a team of student writer/designers who created an online literary arts magazine called *Din*. The students who created *Din* wanted future classes of students to be able to put out new editions of the magazine. They decided to use a wiki for their documentation, which allows all registered users to add to and edit the text. This wiki contains specifics about what design elements (in relation to rhetorical choices) the design group used to distribute different social-media iterations of the magazine on a blog and on Facebook; it also hosts an archive of promotional materials and logo designs. In the future, the documentation wiki could easily be changed as needed.

Figure 8.7 Project Documentation in a Wiki

The project documentation for *Din* illustrates and discusses logo and visual design choices (http://dinguidebook.wikispaces.com).

Process! | Go to *Wikipedia*, search for a term related to your project, and click that entry's "View history" tab to see what kind of changes have happened recently. How do wiki editors comment on their changes on this page?

Delivering Documentation through Comments

A Web site designer will often embed comments into the HTML code to help future designers understand the designer's thought process when creating the site. Comments do not show up on the actual Web page but are viewable in the source code and in Web-editing programs like Dreamweaver or KompoZer. In the comment shown in **Figure 8.8**, the designers of New Mexico State University's Web site provide a purpose for this particular document (an HTML template that other NMSU Web designers can use to retain design consistency across university Web pages) and instructions on how to use and modify the styles provided. For non–Web-based projects, marginal comments in word-processing programs might be similarly used.

```
1  <!DOCTYPE html PUBLIC "-//W3C//DTD XHTML 1.0 Strict//EN" "http://www.w3.org/TR/xhtml1/DTD/xhtml1-strict.dtd">
2  <html xmlns="http://www.w3.org/1999/xhtml" xml:lang="en" lang="en">
3    <head>
4      <title>Department of English at New Mexico State University</title>
5      <meta http-equiv="content-type" content="text/html; charset=iso-8859-1" />
6      <!--
7
8      NMSU CSS-targetable XHTML format template
9      ©2005 NMSU Board of Regents
10
11     Authors:    CC Chamberlin, Phillip Johnson
12     Version:    2.0
13     Date:       2005-09-01
14
15     The purpose of this document is to provide a common format for HTML
16     files so that style sheets can be distributed and updated that can be
17     applied across a wide variety of web documents.  Some extraneous tags
18     are added for future compatibility, and may not be used currently.
19     We've tried to keep the document semantically clean.
20
21     This is the starting point for a document that wants to inherit the
22     look and feel of the NMSU site without having to manually duplicate the
23     page style.  Be aware that if you hack the document structure,
24     future changes to the CSS might cause your hacks to break.  A better
25     approach would be to override the NMSU styles with your own, leaving
26     the document structure alone.
27
28     Special thanks to W3C, A List Apart, Zeldman, CSS Zen Garden, and
29     others who have provided valuable knowledge and examples over the years
30     to make web publishing as clean as it is today.  This document borrows
31     elements from many of these people/organizations.
32
33     -->
34
35     <meta name="author" content="{{ Author }}" />
36     <meta name="Keywords" content="{{ Keywords, comma-delimited }}" />
37     <meta name="Description" content="{{ Description }}" />
38     <meta name="robots" content="all" />
39     <meta name="MSSmartTagsPreventParsing" content="true" />
40
41     <!--
42        Link to the universal NMSU style sheets and the favicon. Note that
43        stylesheets group different styles together; if you need to break
44        things up beyond this, you'll have to use @import and hope that the
45        browser can deal with it.
46     -->
```

Figure 8.8 Comment to Users of Web Templates Embedded in the File's Source Code

Go to a Web site that you used for your project and view its code. (The code is sometimes found under View>Source, or you can search for instructions for finding the source code if it's not readily apparent.) How did the designers of the site use HTML commenting? If they didn't use commenting, are there places where it would have been useful?

Process!

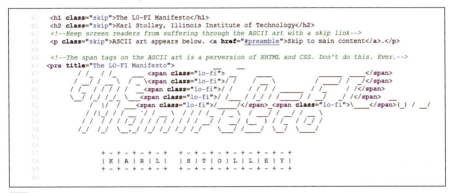

```
40    <h1 class="skip">The LO-FI Manifesto</h1>
41    <h2 class="skip">Karl Stolley, Illinois Institute of Technology</h2>
42    <!--Keep screen readers from suffering through the ASCII art with a skip link-->
43    <p class="skip">ASCII art appears below. <a href="#preamble">Skip to main content</a>.</p>
44
45    <!--The span tags on the ASCII art is a perversion of XHTML and CSS. Don't do this. Ever.-->
46    <pre title="The LO-FI Manifesto">
47        / /_  / /_    ___  <span class="lo-fi"> __                                  ___</span>
48       / _/ / /_  \ / _ \<span class="lo-fi">/ /         /___\              / _/ / /_/</span>
49      / /_ / / / / /   __<span class="lo-fi">-fi">/ /    / / /         ____     / /_    / /</span>
50      \_/ / / /_/_ \___<span class="lo-fi">-fi">/ /__  / / / / /____/ / _7   _/ /</span>
51        / /|/_7 ___<span class="lo-fi">-fi">/____/</span><span class="lo-fi">\___</span>(_) / __/
52        / /\_/ /_  `/ / _ \ / / / / _ 7_ \  / _7 / / / _ \
53       / / 7 / /_7 / / /7 / / /__7 _/   _/ (__  ) / /  / /_7
54      /_/ /_/ \_,_/ /_/ /_/ /_/ /_/    \_7 /___/ \_7 \_/
55
56
57           + - + - + - + - +   + - + - + - + - + - + - + - +
58           | K | A | R | L |   | S | T | O | L | L | E | Y |
59           + - + - + - +     + - + - + - + - + - + - + - +
60
```

Figure 8.9 Source Code Comments Can Provide Help for Future Users

The code for Karl Stolley's "Lo-Fi Manifesto" includes comments that help new designers learn how to borrow code so that they can tweak it for themselves. Visit **bedfordstmartins.com /writerdesigner** to see how that works.

write/design **assignment**

Documenting Your Project

The following structure provides a rough guide that you can use to create a documentation guide for clients or for future users of your project. You can also search for other genres of documentation and analyze their structures and conventions, if your needs are greater than these questions suggest. When writing up your documentation, you should refer back to your proposal and style guide (from Chapter 5) as well as your delivery plan (from earlier in this chapter). All of these documents together will help you form a more sustainable documentation guide for your clients or stakeholders.

- **Overview:** What are the major rhetorical goals of your project?
- **Audience:** Who are the target readers/users/viewers of the project, and what design choices have you made to accommodate them?
- **Design:** What ideas guided your organization of this project? If it's a print text, presentation, or webtext, where should key elements be placed? If it's a video, audio, or animation project, what guidelines can you offer for how elements are ordered, compressed, or edited?
- **Media:** What stylistic considerations are there for images, audio, or video used in the project?

Reporting on Your Final Project

In many classes and workplaces, you may be asked to make a presentation on your completed project. Doing so gives you a chance to show off your hard work and to talk about the many decisions and challenges you faced in creating the project. End-of-project reports can be many different genres, including presentations, written reports, white papers, technical papers, scholarly articles, news features, and less formal genres such as blog posts, reflections, and exit interviews. In any of these genres, you have an opportunity to demonstrate to your audience and stakeholders the value of what you've done and the reasoning that got you to that point. Reflecting on your research and design processes as well as on your final project also allows you to see just how much you've learned and how you might approach your next project differently to make it even stronger and more efficient.

If you are required to report on your multimodal project, keep in mind that your task is to be persuasive, not just descriptive. Help your audience understand each of the major design and rhetorical choices you've made and how those choices were appropriate to your particular rhetorical situation. For example, if your task was to create a flyer to advertise a speaking event (as in **Fig. 8.10**), you could point to the way you used the design choice of contrast to attract readers' attention by placing vividly colored text on a dark background. You could also discuss how this design choice was appropriate for the context because most flyers on a busy bulletin board tend to have a white background; thus this flyer is distinct and stands out. If you were asked to create an audio documentary, you could refer your audience back to the sections of your project in which you incorporated background music or specific sound effects behind your narration to help set a particular mood. No matter what your subject or mode of delivery, discussing why you made the decisions you did will help your audience understand how you attempted to navigate the rhetorical situation.

Here are some questions you should consider when reporting on your multimodal project to your stakeholders or clients:

- What were the **primary ideas and intentions that guided your project**?
- What were the key **rhetorical choices** you made?
  - What was your **purpose** in creating this project?
  - Who was your intended **audience**, and what did you do to attend to their needs or interests?

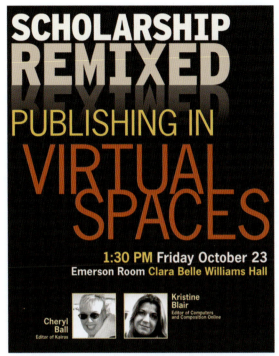

Figure 8.10 A Flyer Advertising a Speaking Event

Design choices for this flyer include large type and contrasting colors so that it will stand out on a bulletin board.

- What **context** did you design this project to be used in, and why?
- How did you select the **genre** that you used for your project?
- What were the key **design choices** you made?
  - How did you make use of emphasis, contrast, organization, alignment, and proximity?
  - What shaped your decisions about how elements of your project were arranged, whether on paper, on-screen, or in video or audio?
- What were your key **modal choices**? Which modes did you use, and why?
- What shaped your **dissemination choices** for how and where you would share your project with your audience?
- What were your most significant **project challenges and successes** as you planned, researched, drafted, and revised your multimodal project?
- What would you do differently if you started over? What lessons did you learn that can be applied to future projects?

Process! | Search for different genres for presenting your final project, such as reports and white papers. How do these documents differ in terms of their genre conventions?

CASE STUDY

Final Reports

Phillip, a student in one of Jenny's classes, designed the "Scholarship Remixed" flyer in **Figure 8.10** (page 133) and was required to write a final report for that project. In the excerpt that follows, you can see how Phillip researched the flyer genre, brainstormed by sketching initial ideas, and worked through the criteria for the assignment to consider the rhetorical situation. His report discusses his design and rhetorical choices, and reflects on his composing process to analyze what worked well and how he might improve both the flyer and his design process in the future.

Preproduction process

I started out thinking about what ideas or images the words might evoke. I gravitated toward the "Scholarship Remixed: Publishing in Virtual Spaces" title because the ideas of remixing and spaces open up lots of possibilities.

I surfed my favorite design sites to look at typefaces and color schemes. I also sketched some drawings to work out the density and hierarchy of the information and to work through a few layout ideas. I decided fairly early on this would be a typographic layout and that I wanted it to be bold in order to stand out from the clutter of a bulletin board.

Rhetorical choices

I suppose the decision to focus on producing a typographic layout is the main rhetorical choice I made. Given that the audience for this presentation is mainly English students, it seemed appropriate to focus on the words and try to find ways to make them interesting without losing readability or clarity. For me, the purpose of a flyer like this is to convince people to show up by focusing on the what, along with the where and when. Toward that end, I made sure that the time and place information is not hidden or ambiguous.

Design principles

Repetition is present in the design and is most apparent in the treatment of the photos and the accompanying text, even though the elements are not exact repeats. Colors also repeat to help unify and balance the design. Alignment is working with the various type elements on a number of levels. Proximity is most obvious in the relationship of the photos to each other and to their accompanying text.

Type

As this was always intended to be a typographic design, I spent a lot of time picking out the typefaces. I used Interstate for the bolder typeface at the top of the design, along with a few variants of News Gothic for everything else. I like the contrast between the two typefaces.

Visit **bedfordstmartins.com/writerdesigner** to see two reflective reports: Phillip's complete report, including his thoughts on the revision process, and Andrew Wasowicz's video reflection from his multimodal class.

write/design assignment

Reporting on Your Project

Analyze what kind of end-of-project report you should create to complete your project and fulfill your clients' needs. Use the questions from the Reporting on Your Final Project section (or others you and your client, boss, or instructor create) and your proposal to produce a final report on your multimodal project for your stakeholders. Your final report might include all of the major texts you've produced as part of this project (depending on the client's needs), and should most definitely include instructions on where the project itself resides or how it will be delivered (e.g., your delivery plan, with metadata) and the project's documentation/ style guides. Make plans to turn in the project to your client or instructor. Then go have fun! You're done!

Credits

2.1	Courtesy of Steve Halle; created for the English Department's Publications Unit at Illinois State University; line art by Melaina Comics
2.2b	Courtesy of Cheryl Ball
2.2d	Courtesy of Cheryl Ball
2.3	© Bettmann/CORBIS
2.4	Courtesy of Cheryl Ball
2.5	PhotoFest, Inc.
2.6	Info@wikimedia.org
2.7–2.10	Courtesy of Washington State University
2.11	Tom O'Toole
2.14	Peter Steiner/The New Yorker Collection. www.cartoonbank.com
3.1–3.2	Courtesy of Angela Buchanan
3.2a	Courtesy of Twitter and Cheryl Ball
3.3	Reproduced with permission of Palgrave Macmillan
3.4	Maria Andersen/Prezi Inc.
3.6	Musicovery
3.7	Courtesy of Edmond Chang
3.8	William Maelia/Prezi Inc.
3.9	© Elyse Canfield
3.10–3.11	Courtesy of Cheryl Ball
4.1	Peter Steiner/The New Yorker Collection. www.cartoonbank.com
4.3	Keith Aoki, James Boyle, and Jennifer Jenkins. http://web.law.duke.edu/cspd/comics
4.4	Courtesy of Ariel Popp
4.4a–4.5	Copyright Creative Commons. Made available by Creative Commons Attribution 3.0 license. http://creativecommons.org
4.6	Courtesy of Martine Courant Rife
4.7	Photo courtesy of Jennifer Sheppard
4.8	"Piled Higher and Deeper" by Jorge Cham. www.phdcomics.com
4.9	Courtesy of Karl Stolley
4.10	DreamWorks/Photofest
4.11	Courtesy of Adam Arola

5.1	Courtesy of freecsstemplates.org. Made available by Creative Commons 3.0 license.
5.2	Courtesy of Ariel Popp
5.3	Courtesy of Casey Kilroy, Erin Lentz, Jess Krist, and Brian Sorenson
5.4	Courtesy of Kristin Arola
5.5	Copyright 2012 by Bob Haarmans. Made available under a Creative Commons Attribution 2.0 license. http://www.flickr.com/photos/rhaarmans/7279652198/
5.6	"Piled Higher and Deeper" by Jorge Cham. www.phdcomics.com
5.7	Project Bamboo
6.1	Courtesy of Nick Winters
6.2	Courtesy of Kristin Arola
6.3	Kenneth Chan
6.4–6.8	Courtesy of Courteney Dowd
6.10–6.14	Courtesy of Jeff Kuure, Elena Duff, and Matt Seigel
6.15	Copyright 2013 by Source, a Knight-Mozilla OpenNews project. Made available by Creative Commons Attribution 3.0 Unported license. http://source.mozillaopennews.org/en-US/articles/how-we-made-snow-fall
7.1–7.2	Biosphoto/Superstock
7.3–7.4	Courtesy of Cheryl Ball
7.5	Shawn Apostel/Prezi Inc.
7.6–7.7	Courtesy of Jeff Kuure, Elena Duff, and Matt Seigel
8.1	Shutterstock
8.3	Courtesy of Ryan Cordell
8.4	Cheryl Ball/Facebook
8.5	StoryCorps, www.storycorps.org
8.6	Wikimedia Foundation
8.7	Courtesy of Jen Almjeld
8.8	Courtesy of CC Chamberlin and Phillip Johnson
8.9	Courtesy of Karl Stolley
8.10	Courtesy of Phillip Johnson

e-Page Credits

E.1	Courtesy of The American Indian College Fund. All rights reserved.
E.2–E.3	Copyright Creative Commons. Made available by Creative Commons Attribution 2.5 license. http://creativecommons.org/videos/wanna-work-together
E.6	"Buyout Footage"
E.8	© Bettmann/CORBIS
E.9	Courtesy of Cheryl Ball
E.10	PhotoFest
E.11–E.12f	Courtesy of Washington State University
E.13	Tom O'Toole
E.15	Peter Steiner/The New Yorker Collection. www.cartoonbank.com
E.19	Joseph Sohm/Visions of America/Corbis
E.22	Maria Andersen/Prezi Inc.
E.24–E.25	Courtesy of Edmond Chang
E.26–E.27	William Maelia/Prezi Inc.
E.28–E.29	Courtesy of Cheryl Ball/Matt Wendling
E.30–E.44	Keith Aoki, James Boyle, and Jennifer Jenkins. http://web.law.duke.edu/cspd/comics
E.46–E.47	*Creative Commons Kiwi* by Creative Commons Aotearoa New Zealand is licensed under a Creative Commons Attribution 3.0 New Zealand (CC BY) license. The video was made with support from InternetNZ and is a project of the Royal Society of New Zealand. Produced by Mohawk Media. http://creativecommons.org/videos/creative-commons-kiwi
E.48	Courtesy of Martine Courant Rife
E.51	Courtesy of Ariel Popp
E.52–E.53	Shawn Apostel/Prezi Inc.
E.54–E.55	Courtesy of Karl Stolley
E.56–E.58	Courtesy of Phillip Johnson
E.59–E.60	Courtesy of Xtranormal and Andrew Wasowicz

Index

Missing something? To access the Bedford Integrated Media that accompanies this text, visit **bedfordstmartins.com/writerdesigner**. Students who do not buy a new book can purchase access to Integrated Media at this site.

Inside the Bedford Integrated Media for *Writer/Designer*

Chapter 1

Text, from *ix: visualizing composition* (tutorial)

Process! Creative Commons, *Wanna Work Together?* (video)

Process! Comparing Gestures in Two Speeches (video)

Chapter 2

Audience, from *ix: visualizing composition* (tutorial)

Purpose, from *ix: visualizing composition* (tutorial)

Context, from *ix: visualizing composition* (tutorial)

Interactive Design Choices Analysis (video)

Emphasis, from *ix: visualizing composition* (tutorial)

Contrast, from *ix: visualizing composition* (tutorial)

Organization, from *ix: visualizing composition* (tutorial)

Alignment, from *ix: visualizing composition* (tutorial)

Proximity, from *ix: visualizing composition* (tutorial)

More Design Terms, from *ix: visualizing composition* (tutorial)

Chapter 3

Maria Andersen, "Playing to Learn?" (prezi)

Edmond Chang, "Gaming Writing: Teaching (with) Video Games" (prezi)

William Maelia, "Using Web-Based Games to Support 21st Century Learning" (prezi)

Matt Wendling's Pitch (video)

Chapter 4

Keith Aoki, James Boyle, Jennifer Jenkins, *Bound by Law?* (comic)

Sample Consent Form (download)

Process! Creative Commons Licenses (video)

Martine Courant Rife, *How to Cite a Cereal Box in MLA 2009* (video)

Process! Classic Movie Credits (video)

Chapter 5

Ariel Popp, Life-Based Web Comics (webtext)

Chapter 6

How We Made Snow Fall (reading)

Chapter 7

Cheryl's Video Feedback (video)

Chapter 8

Karl Stolley, "Lo-Fi Manifesto" Source Code Comments (video)

Phillip's Written Final Report (reading)

Andrew's Video Final Report (video)